How and Why Iowans Named Kossuth County in 1851

Prepared for unveiling Kossuth's statue in Algona, Iowa on July 13, 2001 in commemoration of naming the county after the former Governor of Hungary.

Kossuth was in 1851-1852 the guest of the American Congress. In wider perspective the search for answers became a short study of the human struggle to replace the despotic power of kings with the ballot box power of people longing for democracy.

by

Rezső Ralph Gracza

Beaver's Pond Press, Inc.

Edina, Minnesota

> *About the cover photo*
>
> The inscription on the pedestal reads:
>
> KOSSUTH
> LAJOS (LOUIS) KOSSUTH
> 1802–1894
>
> The namesake of Kossuth County. Kossuth was a Hungarian freedom fighter and leader of the 1848–1849 revolution for Hungarian independence. He was known as one of the greatest statesmen and orators of the mid-19th century. He was a prominent figure, well known in the United States at the time Kossuth County was established on January 15, 1851. Dedicated this 13th day of July, 2001.

How and Why Iowans Named Kossuth County in 1851 ©2001 by Rezső Ralph Gracza

All rights reserved. No part of this book may be reproduced in any form whatsoever, by photography or xerography or by any other means, by broadcast or transmission, by translation into any kind of language, nor by recording electronically or otherwise, without permission in writing from the publisher, except by a reviewer, who may quote brief passages in critical articles or reviews.

Library of Congress Catalog Card Number: 2001091560

ISBN 1-931646-03-1

1. History 2. Kossuth 3. Statues 4. Democracy 5. Heritage 6. Civics

Printed in the United States of America

First Printing: July 2001

04 03 02 01   5 4 3 2 1

Beaver's Pond Press, Inc.

5125 Danen's Drive
Edina, Minnesota 55439-1465
(952) 829-8818
www.beaverspondpress.com

Foreword

In the agenda of the Kossuth County Board of Supervisors and of the Department Heads, the construction items came up of landscaping the area in front of the Courthouse and celebrating the 150th anniversary of the County. In October 1999, the Board approved the "Kossuth on State Project" and appointed Mr. William Farnham to the Chair of the Committee. The subcommittee of the Kossuth County Historical Society was created to administer the project. Engineering planning called for benches to be placed on the patio to be shaped like Kossuth County out of brick pavers, but a symbol was also needed to memorialize the past, present and future of the people living there: families, businesses, government entities and organizations. A full size bronze statue of Louis Kossuth as Champion of Liberty was chosen for this symbol. 150 years ago Kossuth was chosen in naming the County. The statue was made by Mr. Wayne E. Thompson of Swea City Iowa , a sculptor, who does his own bronze casting. Since 1979 he has cast over 50 pieces representing Midwest themes. The members of the Kossuth on State project and volunteers spent many hours preparing the celebration of unveiling the statue on July 13, 2001. The celebration was indeed a historical event in Kossuth County.

The unveiling of Kossuth's statue may not make the news program on the TV screen, but the spirit of those who named the County, and the spirit of those who 150 years later commemorated democratic ideals, have historical importance. They cherished the democratic heritage of Kossuth, who left a permanent legacy to the people of the United States.

I am indebted to Mrs. Ruth Bartels of the State Historical Society of Iowa, Mrs. Lisa F. Leibfacher of the Ohio Historical Center and Engineers Richard Schiek and Doug Miller of Kossuth County Historical Society, who provided much of the information used in this booklet. Special thanks is extended to Dr. David Kopf, professor emeritus of the History Department of the University of Minnesota, who undertook the work of edition including the clarity of the language.

Thank you.

Rezső Ralph Gracza
Minnetonka, June 7, 2001

Table of Contents*

1. Introduction 1

1.1, 1.2	Human aspiration in leadership. – The Greek and Roman examples.
1.3	The revival of human aspirations in the pre–19th century.
1.4	The aspirations 150 years ago. – Their struggles for democracy in historical perspectives.

2. What happened in France? 3

2.1, 2.2	Philosophers affect Europe's governmental systems.
2.3, 2.4, 2.5	Unrests about "who should pay taxes?" – The seizure of the Bastille
2.6, 2.7	The fall of the "ancient regime." – Civil Constitution for the clergy. – What happened to King Louis XVI?
2.8, 2.9	The anti–despotic clubs. – The First Republic.
2.10, 2.11	The French Revolutionary Wars. – The rise and fall of Napoleon.
2.12	The Vienna Congress and its failure.
2.13	Achievements by 1835 in the struggle for democracy.
2.14, 2.15	Economic, demographic developments and "gloire" bring back the kings. – The Second Republic sends the kings into exile.
2.17	In 1852 the divided French society votes back Prince Louis Napoleon.
2.18	This review ends in 1852.

3. What happened in the Habsburg lands? 9

3.1	Hungary's struggle with the Habsburg dynasty.
3.2	The background of Louis Kossuth.
3.3, 3.4, 3.5	The rise of Kossuth to lead the Opposition on the Hungarian Diets.
3.6	The power structure in Vienna. – The members of the Kamarilla.
3.7, 3.8	A volley on the people starts the Revolution in Vienna. – The Kamarilla dismisses Metternich and Apponyi.
3.9	Emergency declared. – Governor Windischgräts shoots with cannon on insurgents.
3.10, 3.11, 3.12, 3.13, 3.14	"The Pest Youth" drafts a Resolution on the wishes of the Hungarian Nation – It is read at public rallies. – The City Council and the Governor accept the demands in the "Resolution".
3.15, 3.16, 3.17	The Diet in Pozsony accepts Kossuth's Manifesto. – King Ferdinand V sanctions it in Vienna.

* In lieu of an index

3.18	President Batthyány presents the first Independent Hungarian Ministerium to the Diet in Pest.
3.19, 3.20	The dynasty intrigues its subjects against its Hungarian subjects.
3.21	In Zagreb "Governor" Jellasics is celebrated. – Proponents of Illyria formulate a Croatian Manifesto.
3.22, 3.23, 3.24	In Újvidék the Serbian orthodox communities formulate a petition for a Voivodina within the Habsburg domain. – Archbishop Rajasics calls a meeting In Karlóca, that elects a patriarch and a despot.
3.25	Pan–Slavic reverend Hurban in Liptó–Szent–Miklós writes an Order to the Slovak populace to disobey the government in Pest.
3.26, 3.27	Reconstructing Dacia from Transylvania, Moldova and Wallachia Orthodox bishop Saguna proposes a kingdom for a Romanov ruler. – The religious meeting in Balázsfalva formulates a petition and pays homage to the king. – Abrudbánya ravaged by Janku.
3.28	Kossuth averts the financial machinations of the Kamarilla.
3.29, 3.30	Ferdinand V revokes his decisions. – But scared dynasty members publicly sanction them in Pozsony.
3.31	The Hungarian National Army and the National Bank are created.
3.32	Archduke Stephen, General Móga and Jellasics meet in a camp at Siófok.
3.33	In Budapest on the route to dissolve the Diet, the mob beats to death the Austrian Commander–in–chief.
3.34	At Pákozd the Croatian army is defeated.
3.35	King Ferdinand V resigns in favor of Francis Joseph. – Hungary's independence movement is "de jure" annulled.
3.36	The imperial army occupies Budapest. – The Diet moves to Debrecen. – Batthyány meets Windischgräts at Bicske.
3.37	At Kápolna the National army defeats the Imperial forces. – The Kremsier Document. – Walden replaces Windischgrätz.
3.38	In Debrecen the Diet dethrones the Habsbug dynasty.
3.39	The imperial army retreats. – The costly occupation of Buda by Görgei.
3.40	Dynastic politics sends Francis Joseph to Warsaw. – He asks Czar Nicholas for militay help. – The Russians invade Hungary.
3.41	Hungary is abandoned by the West.
3.42	The perky General, Görgey and the Governor, Kossuth.
3.43	Russian General Paskievics overwhelms the Hungarian Army. – At Temesvár Hungary looses a major battle. – At Arad Görgei surrenders to the Russians. – Kossuth flees to Turkey.
3.44	The execution of Batthyány in Budapest and of 13 Hungarian generals in Arad.
3.45	Kossuth and his family.

3.46, 3.47	The Sultan frees the Hungarian prisoners of war. – Kossuth boards the US frigate, Mississippi, to visit in America.
3.48	Kossuth stops to visits in England. – Kossuth speaking the language of Shakespeare. – On December 5, 1851 Kossuth arrives to the US.

4. What happened in the Republic of the United States? 25

4.1, 4.2	The American elite watches closely the events in the "only other Republic of the World"
4.3	The first refugees of the Hungarian War of Independence in Decatour County, Iowa.
4.4, 4,5	Rev. Tefft lectures about Hungary and Kossuth. – W. Dennison invites Tefft to speak to the Ohio General Assembly.
4.6	Resolutions passed by the Ohio General Assembly.
4.7	Tefft assembles his lectures into a book.
4.8	President Fillmore invites Kossuth to visit America as the "Nation's Guest". – Kossuth's famous words about democracy.
4.9	Kossuth, the invited politician. – His effect on the US populace.
4.10	Supporters of slavery versus the abolitionists.
4.11	The goal of Kossuth's visit in America. – The failure of his mission.
4.12	Louis Kossuth versus Orestes Brownson.
4.13	Monied interest did not side with Kossuth.
4,14	A sympathetic leader in the Western world. – Kossuth's permanent legacy to the United States. – Quotes from US notables.
4.15	Contemporary opinion about Kossuth as formulated by Horace Greeley.
4.16	Kossuth's popularity rising into a mania.
4.17	Kossuth's ideas and popularity that led to name a county after him.

5. Bibliography 33

6. Illustrations 37

1. Introduction

1.1　In the art of leadership the leader must acknowledge the **aspirations of people,** who support him. In history the modes of leadership have varied widely: - the rule of monarchs over the subjects, - the rise of politically responsible persons in democratic societies, and the rule of dictators, who control the populace by totalitarian means. - It was found by archeologists, that some *primitive form of democracy was practiced even in prehistoric times*. The innate, strong human aspirations for independence blossomed in the governments of the Greek city states. The Greeks practiced *"direct democracy"*, in which representatives responsible to their electorates obtained power to administer public affairs. - In Rome the system of governance, breastfed on Greek examples, was not so lucky. The Roman government may be called an *"oligarchic republic"* or the rule by the few chosen by the senate with a strong military to take care of the extended Roman empire.

1.2　These forms of "successful" governments sunk gradually into **oblivion over the period since the fourth century A.D.** During this *period of "Heroes and Kings"*, peoples of Europe had to live with the hardship and fear caused by the "great migration". In this period developed the kingdoms, as we know them today. But the *human aspirations* for individual freedom did not die, as the *coal of fire remained alive* seething under the ash of oppression. - People longed for the "good old Roman times"; a German ruler even took the title of Roman emperors.

1.3　**In pre-19th century,** strengthened by technical and economic fermentation **the coal of fire burst into flame** in the bloody French Revolution of 1789-1899. At the same time with the advantages of geography and without strong historic traditions, *America succeeded in shaking off oppressive despotism*. It took about six years, 1775-1781, while fighting for their freedom with help of the French against the common enemy of England. The help contributed to the near bankruptcy of the French state finances. On a new continent the Americans established a republic on the Graeco-Roman model, the only one in the world at that time. - *After about 1600 years the human aspiration for democracy came to the surface again.*

1.4   To understand what people 150 years ago were concerned with beyond their everyday routine, a **historical review** is presented describing in sufficient detail about what was happening in the world. It was from Europe, that most of the people came in the US. Many of them still nursed family connections in the old world. I shall attempt to roll back the pages of history 150 years ago in order to acquaint the reader with the perceptions and motivations, that shaped events. In this endeavour I will be assisted *by the electronic telegraph and printed newspapers* like the "Liberator", a Boston weekly, or the "National Era" a Washington weekly, both in the years of 1851 and 1852.

2. What happened in France?

2.1　　It was less simple **in Europe,** where the power image of kings and despots had deep traditional roots next to the power of the clergy. It became disappointing that by the bloody misdeeds of the French revolution **the flame of human aspiration sputtered** and finally was put out by another despot, Napoleon. But in the chain of events he became a *national hero*, who was finally removed from power by an alliance of despots bringing back again *the absolute power of kings, who ruled in the name of God.*

2.2　　Popular concepts of the public in the 2nd half of the 18th century were greatly influenced by revered **thinkers, philosophers**, such as Descartes, Spinoza, Locke etc. While suggesting different routes for the happiness of the human race, *all converged on the dignity and social status of the common people.* Some of them, like Montesquieu, Voltaire, Russeau were less abstract and urged trying out their ideas in practice.

2.3　　Upon the upswing of technical developments in Europe over the period from 1715 to 1800 France's poulation doubled; **France became Europe's most populous country**; 26 million people in 1789. Generally, public administration became more complex and expensive. To produce the needed funds, to get rid of budget deficits, *paying taxes were extended to the aristocracy and clergy.* This first happened in England. All the privileged classes reacted by revolting against such taxes, thereby increasing the public discontent already high because of food shortages caused by crop failures. – Note, that the American Revolution was also sparked by refusing to pay taxes imposed by the king of England and was also predating major events of the French revolution.

2.4　　In the spring and summer in **1788** there were **unrests** in Paris, Grenoble. Dijon, Toulouse, Pau and Rennes about taxes. *Sould taxes be paid by the "third estates" or by the nobility/clergy of France?* In the 1789 January–May general election the *burgeoisie and aristocracy* split in the middle: out of 1200 seats 600 were won by the third estate, 300 by the nobility and 300 by the clergy.

2.5　　Excited by the perhaps false news of aristocratic conspiracy on **July 14, 1789,** the tension between the burgeoisie and aristocracy exploded when *the people of Paris* **seized**

the Bastille, the symbol of despotism. On August 4 the National Assembly *abolished the feudal regime and the tithe*, taxes paid by the unprivileged populace. On August 26, following the examples of the American revolutionaries, the *"Declaration of the Rights of Man and the Citizen"* was issued claiming liberty, equality, inviolability of property and the right to resist oppression. King Louis XVI refused to sanction. On October 5 the people of Paris marched to the royal palace in Versailles and the next day they brought back the royal family to Paris. They became hostages in the Tuilleries garden.

2.6   The Constitutional Assembly worked till September **1791 on the constitition** completing the abolition of feudalism, suppressing the "old orders", establishing *civil equality (only in metropolitan France; slavery was retained in the colonies)*, establishing rights of eligibility for public office. Nationalizing the land of the church to pay off the public debt led to a widespread redistribution of property. The burgeoisie, the peasant landowners and share croppers were the chief beneficiaries.

2.7   The assets of the church were confiscated and the clergy received salaries from the State. The clergy became regulated by a **Civil Constitution,** which was **rejected by the Pope**. The conflict between the Church and State led to a schism in the church aggravating the violence attending the changes. The "ancient regime" was swept away. *France was organized into Departments,* the districts were adminstered by elected assemblies. Jurisdiction was administered by elected judges. The Constitutional Assembly tried to create a monarchical regime (that had slowly developed in England), where the legislative and executive powers were shared between the king and the assembly. This body was elected biannually by the "active citizens"; i.e. Frenchmen, who paid more than a certain amount of tax. – Abhorred by the Civil Constitution for the clergy and listening to his aristocratic advisors, on *June 20–21, 1791 the king tried to flee the country, but was stopped in Varennes and brought back to Paris.*

2.8   The French events left no hope for the revolutionaries in the United Province (Habsburg Netherland), Belgium and Switzerland. People bent for changes in England, Ireland, Germany, **Austrian lands,** Italy etc. *sympathized with the French Revolution forming clubs*, masonic lodges and *demonstrating for concessions on the streets*. The rulers became really worried, when the Constituent Assembly proclaimed the revolutionary principle of international law: i.e. *self determination*. With the persecution of the French–liking "Jacobines" international tension increased, finally *on April 20, 1792* **France declared war on Austria and Prussia**, where the French emigrés, who had left home during the Revolution, were asking other European governments for their reinstatement in France.

2.9   Incited again by the rumor of an aristocratic conspiracy **on August 10, 1792** the revolutionaries led by the Jacobines in Paris **occupied the Tuilleries,** massacred the imprisoned nobles and clergy and imprisoned the king in the Temple. *The king fled to the Assembly*. – On the day of **September 20, 1792,** when the newly elected Assembly Convention first met, the Prussian army was also checked by the French army at Valmy.

Next day the Convention *proclaimed the abolition of the monarchy and the establishment of the* **(First) Republic.**

2.10   Meanwhile in Paris, *terror ravaged* the aristocracy, the clergy and the revolutionaries themselves; Louis XVI was beheaded and he **French Revolutionary Wars, 1792–1799,** went on in several phases. At the beginning Austria, Prussia and Great Britain fought in a coalition. Napoleon became popular and politically powerful from his military successes. When the Convention was still debating another new constitution, **Napoleon** asking for power, *the Assembly was dissolving.*

2.11   The French Revolutionary Wars, the Napoleonic war engagements, including expeditions to Egypt and Syria, the Russian campaign, kept changing also the political landscape. While Napoleon's successes earned for the *French the national "gloire"*, they had also to deal with the **defeat of Napoleon on June 18, 1815 at Waterloo.** He was exiled by the victorious allied powers to the island of Elba in the Atlantic.

2.12   After the Napoleonic era**, the Congress of Vienna, 1814–1815**, reorganized Europe. By some, the settlement was considered the most comprehensive treaty Europe had in recent history. Not understanding the demands of the age, while acting with some benevolence, the Congress failed. The quadruple alliance of Austria, Prussia, Russia and Great Britain kept the "initiative" in their hands. Their *four ministers decided the future of the conquered territories and communicated it to France and Spain*. With confidence that the throne and clergy had strong traditional roots, the *restoration brought back the church as well as the monarch*. Under the direction of the Austrian Metternich they reestablished the former despised systems. – *The flame of human aspirations had to retreat again to the seething coal under the ash of oppression and neglect.*

2.13   But the coal under the ash was made warmer by many other events. Britain started to lose America in 1783; in 1807 Britain was just to abolish the slave trade in the entire empire; in 1833 Britain abolished slavery as an institution; Spain and Portugal lost their empire in South and Central America; by 1825, sheltered by the Monroe doctrine, Latin Americans won their independence; the British traded and ruled in India, the Dutch in Java spreading over Indonesia; in 1830 the Greek won independence from Turkey; in 1827 Britain intervened in Portugal to preserve the form of constitutional government; **in 1830** a group raised the French tricolor flag of the Revolution; **king Charles** fled to England and **was replaced by Louis Philippe of the Orleans** branch of the Capet French royal family; *the system in France resembled to a limited constitutional monarchy;* in 1830 the Belgians won their independence from the Dutch, that violated some provision of the Vienna Congress' settlement. – Ripples of revolutions stirred by such events spread even to lands under the watchful eyes and heavy hands of Metternich. In the states of the *German Confederation, local revolts forced concessions from reluctant rulers*. In 1832 in a Frankfurt meeting Prussia and Austria passed the **"six acts"** curbing press and opposition in all German states. Thus in *1835 Metternich's system ruled again in Germany*. In Italy Modena,

Parma and the papal territories faced revolts, which were quickly quelled by Austria. Only in free Switzerland did not Metternich succeed, where the Cantons set up rather liberal constitutions.

2.14   The post-Napoleonic kings Louis XVIII, Charles X and Louis Philippe lost the confidence of their parliaments. Its dissolution in 1830 precipitated the successful **"three day revolution"** in Paris, that sent Charles to exile to London bringing Louis Philippe to the throne. He had to wrestle with **three major parties: the Legitimists, Bonepartists and the Republicans,** all vying for supremacy. This **caused the insurrections of 1836 and 1840,** which attempted to bring **back Louis Napoleon to the throne.** – Among the parties the Republicans appered to be dangerous to the monarchy. – Starting in 1820 they had been well organized; in 1830 a decree drove them underground. In their secret societies supported also by political exiles, they were active, fomenting discontent and outbreaks of which the 1834 and 1840 risings in Paris and Lyon were the most serious. Louis Philippe's ministers headed by *Guizot had to face numerous crises.* – Industrialization since 1820 had gained considerable momentum with the attending low living conditions of the urbanized workers. The *new proletariat was practically left alone in the laissez faire policy of the government,* to select many prophets, theorists, among them *pre–Marxian communists and Christian socialists*, who propounded their *ideas* in coopereatives and also in writings. – The 1846 potato crop failure initiated food supply shortage, raised the price of flour and the year 1847 became "the year of dear bread". The purchasing power of money declined, the depression in agriculture was followed by the depression in industrial production and in finances. This *led to a crisis,* that was aggravated by overspeculation in railway investment, corruption in high places and unpopular foreign policy in Algeria, Egypt and the Bosporus, the "Eastern Question". To deal with these problems, a new movement for *parliamentary reform, the "banquets campaign"* was launched.

2.15   On February 22, 1848 the **"banquet campaign"** was to meet at the parliament, but was banned. On that day, the cowd demonstrated for the dismissal of the unpopular Guizot. *Barricades and red flags appeared in the working class' district.* Louis Philippe was alarmed. To placate the demonstarators he *dismissed Guizot.* The affair appeared to have been settled, but on the next day the troops incidentally fired on the crowd and the temper of populace exploded leading to **the 1848 insurrection**. Next day Louis Philippe (76) abdicated to his ten years old son and went to England in exile. The revolutionaries forgot about the monarchy and **declared the Second Republic**.

2.16   The leaders of *The Second Republic, 1848–1852,* mostly lawyers and journalists, set up their provisional goverment in the Hotel de Ville. Against expectation, their activity *was eminently pacific*. – They realized, that abolishing slavery in the colonies might set Europe ablaze in a new revolutionary crusade for emancipation chasing the socialist utopia of some of their leaders. *Their ideas* centered around universal suffrage for Frenchman over the age of 21, social and economic transformations, replacing the tricolor by the red flag, reducing working hours, proclamation of the right to work, reducing unemployment etc.

Their March decree *increased the French electorate from about 200,000 to 9,000,000,* many of whom in spite of the 1833 education laws and growth of the press, were illiterate. In their chambers the Radical–Socialists won only 100 seats out of 876 representing only an urban minority. – The conflict between the right to work, the unemployment due to economic changes and continuous revolutionary activity promoted *disorder and led to the* **June 23–26, 1848 Insurrection.** The mob sympathizing with the exasperated hungry workers making *unrest less of a political action, than a class war with political consequences,* such as discrediting socialism while considering the abolition of private property. It alarmed the middle and upper classes leading to restriction of liberties granted earlier. Hosts of clubs were placed under supervision, new press laws were introduced, workhours were again lengthened. Socially the *new laws intensified the cleavage between the proletariat and the rest of French society.*

2.17   The parliament at work on the constitution of the **Second Republic faced basic problems.** It insisted, that next to the election of parliamentary representatives the president also be elected by *universal suffrage;* it devised no rules for resolving any conflict between legislative and executive powers creating *loopholes for skilful politicians.* **Prince Louis Napoleon,** for example spent most of his life out of France, but had been chosen deputy by a number of departments, districts in by–election earlier in the year. *By skilful posturing* and by the influence of his magic name, which stood for order, glory and prosperity and by his clever propaganda helping the growth of the Napoleonic legend, in the election for presidency he received an overwhelming majority. *His election in 1852 was the complete overthrow of the republic. It was his mission as a leader to restore the Empire.*

2.18   Focusing on causes and motivation, the chain of coherent revolutionary events and causes were described up to our cutoff in the year of 1852, as they dramatically developed in France. They affected somewhat events motivated similarly in other countries. *It is written in sufficient details necessary to* **explain the motivation and complexity** teaching the cognoscenti and others in selecting the forms of governance and their leaders.

3. What happened in the Habsburg Lands?

3.1 Background. *The Habsburg emperors of Austrian ethnicity were also crowned kings of Hungary.* They made maximum use of the traditional independent Hungarian kings' constitutional rights, but neglected their duties toward Hungarian subjects. They used every opportunity to deprive the nation of its character, its language, preferring instead a policy of assimilation to the German culture. – Since 1526, when the Turks had defeated the Hungarians in the battle of Mohács, **Hungarian independence efforts were suppressed:** Zrinyi and Frangepán were beheaded, Bocskay was poisoned, Thököly, Rákóczy died in exile. *Joseph II*, 1780–1790, intending to modernize the government replaced the counties with ten districts and banned the Hungarian language in public life. He chose not to be crowned to avoid his obligation by oath as the Hungarian king. Instead, he preferred to *assign Hungary to a colonial status.* Meanwhile the 1790 Diet's X. Chapter kept alive the notion of autonomy for Hungarian kings, but all such efforts were circumvented. This *state of affairs convinced many, that the only hope for independence was military action.*

3.2 Perhaps the best known Hungarian statesman, kossuthi és udvardi **Louis Kossuth** was born on October 19, 1802 in the little town of Monok in Hungary's Zemplén county. See his portrait on page 39. His family was ennobled by king Béla IV in the 13th century. The members of his family's Lutheran branch were active in the affairs of Zemplén county. His lawyer father, László was the manager of the manorial estate of Count Andrássy family's holdings in Zemplén county. Sarolta Weber, daughter of the postmaster in Lissza, was his mother. Young Kossuth studied six years in the Újhely Piarist gymnasium. Being the top student of his class, he tutored others contributing his earning to his father. As a student he spoke Latin and became familiar with French and German. He continued his studies in Sárospatak. After he received his law degree in Eperjes, he started his practice. He frequently visited in the county conventions and *because of his thorough knowledge of law, he bacame locally well known.*

3.3 To avoid local envious enemies in 1830 *he became the representative of Countess Szapáry and other nobles in the 1832 Diet in Pozsony.* There he organized the young reformers attending the Diet and **published the "Diet's Bulletin"** written by hands, copied by 40 young friends, to avoid censorship. After the Diet in Pozsony ended, he continued his work in Pest editing his **"Municipal Informations"**. Because of its outspoken language it was banned by the regime upsetting the counties' leadership. To stop his rising popularity in 1937 he was anyway *arrested and put to jail for four years.* He used the time to learn English, reading Shakespeare.

3.4   The imprisonment had a terrible effect on Kossuth's health as was the case with others, who were jailed in the same dungeon such as baron Miklós Wesselényi, who lost his sight and László Lovassy, who lost his mind. – *The 1840 demonstration on behalf of reforms forced the government to concessions* including the permit for a political daily issued to the publisher, Landerer. When Kossuth got out of the jail, May 13, 1840, *Landerer offered him the editorship of his new political daily.* On December 29, 1840 the first issue of the **"Pesti Hírlap"** came out. It soon had more than 5000 subscriber; a success at that time. *It became the herald of liberal reformers.*

3.5   *With his radical views* of advocating Hungary's national sovereignty and liberating Hungary from the Habsburg empire, *he came into conflict with the "father " of the Hungarian Reform, Count István Széchenyi.* He wished to strengthen the country economically first, leading ultimately to the common final goal of independence. *The government* alarmed by Kossuth's daring style of leadership, *forced him out of the editorship* by intrigue. Deeply disappointed, he moved with his family to Tinnye to retire from politics. But his house was inundated by radical reformers urging him to return to Pest, what he ultimately did. – This time *he criticized the regime's custom policy,* which favored the Austrian industry. The Austrians received from Hungary cheap row materials, selling back the products at high price. He founded the Protective Association to advance the cause of Hungarian industry and manufacturing against the more advanced Austrian rival. **By 1847 Kossuth became the accepted leader of the Opposition also on the Diet, as the deputy of Pest county.**

3.6   **The power structure in Vienna.** The Habsburg leaders living the luxurious life of the nobility ruled from the Burg in Vienna, where the decisions were made within an *informal group* nicknamed sardonically **The Kamarilla**, little cubby hole, by writer Jókai. In 1848 its members were: King **Ferdinand V**, (55) of delicate health when he was crowned in 1835. He ruled under the quiet guardianship of his uncle, **archduke Ludwig** (64) and later **archduke Francis Charles** (46). The latter's wife, **archduchess Sophia** (43), was also an influential member of the Kamarilla. She was the daughter of Bavarian king, Joseph Maximilian. She was the sharp and ambitious mother of four sons. She affected all decisions of the State, especially those in dynastic affairs. **Archduke Stephen** (31), when younger he spent time in Alcsúth participating in Hungarian public affairs; in 1848 he was elected Palatine, Governor of Hungary. – Other **archdukes**, like **Johannes Baptist,** (66) **Albrecht** (31), **Williams** (21) were utilized, when needed. – But the head of the Kamarilla was State Chancellor, **Prince Lothar Venczel Metternich** (77), an experienced diplomat of the Congress of Vienna, serving well the dynasty with his absolutistic concepts and dominant personal superiority. His advice was sought and for most of the time followed by the other members. Rich Hungarian aristocrat, **Count György Apponyi** (40), Deputy

Chancellor from 1845, became unpopular at home. To serve the Kamarilla, he appointed administrators arbitrarily over the protesting Hungarian county leadership. – A substantial role was played by **Count Francis Kolowrat** (70), an able administrator, who has been also supporter of Czech cultural and national revival. A well received and well rewarded guest in the court was the easy going, accommodating **Count Joseph Jellasics** (39), a favorite of archduchess Sophia and the dynasty. He was an exponent of Illyrianism, the early Croatian form of nationalism, dreaming about a Southern Slavic imperium within the Habsburg domain.– The Kamarilla had many other supporters, or sycophants and more importantly informers (snitches) in the Habsburg lands, who used the opportunity to shine in the luxurious life of the Vienna court. The Kamarilla was well informed and commanded a variety of tools to enforce its decisions.

3.7   The March 13 revolution in Vienna. In March 1848 news came about riots in Prague, Gracz and Brunn; on March 2, riots broke out in Munich, on March 3, in Nassau, on March 7, in Meiningen–Sachsen, on March 10, in Oldenburg, in Koburg–Sachsen, in Gotha. These riots led to concessions without spilling blood. – On March 13 in Vienna at a demonstration a physician, Adolf Fisher, talked to the crowd also about old–fashioned, senile members of the regime, who were unable and unwilling to listen to their subjects. *Two medical students, Goldner and Putz read to the crowd the March 4th parliamentary address of Kossuth in the of Pozsony Diet.* The crowd became very excited and started to march toward the "Burg" joined by a student delegation. Together they found there in the reception room of marshal Montecuccoli the delegates of the clergy, of the municipal boards and of the Status Militia, all *waiting for an audience with the king, but stalled by the marshal.* The demonstrators filled up the courtyard and the corridors.

3.8   Upon the unexpected appearance of **the military entering into the scene the crowd exploded.** *The front line of the marchers were pelted by stones.* The commanding captain was hit by a brick. He fell to the cobble stone pavement his head bleeding profusely. A volley on the unarmed demonstrators spilled more blood infuriating the crowd. The revolutionay battle spread across the city. – Behind the walls of the Burg protected by the military, the State Council held an emergency session. *Metternich advocated,* that no reforms are needed, the people and the street will quiet down, if the agitators are forcefully removed, the diet in Pozsony should be dissolved, the military should focus on protecting the Burg and should be fortified by additional Czech and Moravian troops. – Upon aggressively entering into the reception room of Archduke Ludwig *an officer of the Status Militia suggested, that the revolution will diffuse, if* **Metternich,** *so hated on the streets, will resign.* Cornered, **the dynasty decided to sacrifice him and his deputy, Apponyi.** Their dismissal was announced to the crowd by archduke Johann. This took out the wind from the sails of street fights. Metternich had to flee in disguise ending up in a London exile.

3.9   March 14th in Vienna. People of the town expected some constitutional declaration. Instead, an **emergency declaration** could be read on the corner posters stating, that the ruler, Ferdinand V appointed Prince Lieutenant General Windischgrätz to the post of

Governor, investing him with full political and military power to reconstitute the law and public order. This *increased the ferocity of street fighting against the cannons of his artillery.*

3.10   Pest, March 14. Encouraged by the successful demonstrations in the German States and in the Habsburg lands also by the news of the bloody Paris revolution, that had driven Louis Philippe from his throne giving rise to the Second French Republic; the *"March Youth" of Pest* led by Petőfi, Vasvári, Irinyi, Irányi, Jókay, Egressy, Klauzál etc. jurists, doctors, writers, actors, prepard a draft *formulating the aspirations of the Hungarian nation.* On March 14 the 12 points of their **Resolution** draft were read and explained by Irinyi on a **public rally** in the hall of the "Opposition Club" of Louis Batthyány. The crowd overflowing from the hall to the street received it in standing ovation especially appreciating its last item the "Union with Transylvania". – This was the first open meeting in Hungarian history, where free citizens of the country were harmonizing in their otherwise divided society. – The rally ended at 6.30 pm. and the crowd dispersed. – Then news came with the late ship from Pozsony about the Vienna revolution and the dismissal of Metternich and Apponyi by the Kamarilla. This caused *great excitement in the café Pilvax*, nicknamed later Szabadságcsarnok (Freedom Hall). With the revolution raging in nearby Vienna, the young reformers felt, that the time arrived to act. In the ensuing feverish discussion they refined the Resolution *deciding about a demostration next day* involving the university youth.

3.11   Pest, March 15, Wednesday. It was a cold day in Pest with rain and snow. Checking once more the text of the Resolution Petőfi, Vasvári Jókai and Bulyovszky posted a handwritten copy on the street corner. The demonstrators filled the café Pilvax and the street nearby. *Reading the Resolution* Jókai told to the crowd, that the nation should insist on these rightful demands. After the ensuing ovation Petőfi presented for the first time his new poem, the *"National Song".* The enthusiastic demonstartors then marched to pick up the students at the medical, engineering, law, liberal art colleges and *Petőfi led* the growing crowd to the *press–shop to print the Resolutions and his poem.* In front of the shop and with a crowd of about 10,000 behind him, Petőfi asked the owner, **Landerer to print them.** Without the censor's approval, he refused to do so. *Petőfi* argued, that the people do not recognize any more the censor. Then Irinyi following Landerer's whispered suggestion, *seized the largest printing press in the name of the people*. At 11.30 am. a copy of the Resolution, the first product of a free press, was ready to be followed by many other copies. The cheering and ovation barely quieted down, when Petőfi appeared in the door with the print of the National Song in his hand. Upon demand he recited it again and afterward the crowd was dismissed.

3.12   The demonstrators gathered again rallying **at 3.00 pm. in front of the National Museum**. *Irinyi read and explained the significance of the Resolution and Petőfi recited the fifth time the National Song,* with the crowd thundering its refrain: "We will not be prisoners any more!" The first two documents of the free press were promptly deposited in the archives of the Museum by director Kubinyi. Next, 6 delegates were selected to induce the

City Magistrate to join the Resolution. With the help of the deputy mayor, *Rottenbiller*, responsible for law and order in the city, the Council voted to accept the Resolution with the condition, that the revolutionaries form a **"Law and Order Committee"**. He volunteered to head the 14 member committee. The Council also decided, that the 12 points of the Resolution be sent to the Diet in Pozsony and to the king in Vienna in form of a petition.

3.13   To seek the **approval of the country's Governor**, a committee, mostly made up of the members of the Law and Order group, was sent to Buda followed by many demonstrators. They marched to the Governor's Court along the cannons and burning wicks prepared by the military to quell a possible revolution. *They found the Council in session.* The committee was invited to sit down at the green table, whereas the demonstrators occupied the courtyard and the corridors. The terrified members of *the Council*, afraid of bloody conflict as in Paris and Vienna, *sanctioned the Resolution,* removed the censors, declared the freedom of press and released the status prisoners. The regular army was not to interfer, as the city of Pest had already its own institution to maintain law and order. The presiding temporary president of the council, Count Zichy Ferenc himself formulated *the document directing the authorities in Pest* and gave it to the committee to deliver to the city hall. *Status prisoner, writer Mihail Stáncsics was immediately released from the dungeon* at the Fehérvári gate. Demonstrators carried him back to Pest in a torchlight procession. When they arrived to the National Theater, the crowd interrupted the play of Bánk Bán and wished to hear again the National Song; this time from Gábor Egressy. Upon demand of the cheering audience completely filling the theater, the members of the delegation in Buda had to recount the daily events.

3.14   In the name of the Pest community 13 leaders of the day issued a **document about the March 15 events.** It notified the nation about *what was obtained in other countries sheddig the blood of citizens, in Budapest it was achieved piecefully by legal understanding within 24 hours.* The City Council opened its doors at 3.00 pm. to a **public meeting**, that **accepted a Resolution** on matters the Diets since 1790 could not settle, sending the Resolution's 12 points to the diet in Pozsony. See pages 40–41.

3.15   Kossuth participated **in the 1847–1848 Diet** in Pozsony as the delegate of Pest county. As l**eader of the opposition**, he sought to formulate the aspirations of the Hungarian nation in a document, **"Opposition Manifesto"** against a substantial number of the privileged nobility and the clergy. Kossuth with the help of Palatine, archduke Stephen, forced the hands of the upper house's magnates and on the 14th of March *the Diet accepted Kossuth's "address to the throne", his Manifesto.*

3.16   The **delivery of the Manifesto,** a document similar to the Resolutions of the people in Pest **to the king**. – On March 15 a delegate of 72 diet members led by Kossuth traveled to Vienna, where they were cheerfully received by the people. On the 16th they were received by Ferdinand V in the throne hall. The Palatine handed the document to *the king,* *who accepted it speaking a few words in broken Hungarian, but with smiling reluctance without any definite promises.* Late in the evening in the Burg, in presence of the Palatine, archduke Francis Charles, Batthyány, Kossuth and Eszterházy Pál, upon the mediation of archduke Stephen and the transmission of news from Pest, *Ferdinand V signed the Manifesto and arranged for the creation of the independent Hungarian cabinet.* Batthyány Lajos was selected as its president. Kossuth did not wish to be a cabinet member, but on the insistence of Batthyány and the Palatine, he accepted the post of the finance minister. – The three leaders leaving the castle joined their Hungarian and Viennese friends, telling them about the day's events. They all continued to pay homage to the king. *On the street one could hear: "Long live the the emperor, long live Batthyány, the Minister President of Hungary!"*

3.17   The next day the delegation returned to Pozsony. In the enthusiastic celebration, Kossuth gave thanks to the Palatine, and Batthyány asked for the confidence of the people. Next day *before the Diet concluded its session, formulated in details the parliamentary duties of the cabinet's ministers.* They coordinated the Kossuth's Manifesto with the 12 points in the Resolution received from the "law and order" delegates from Pest, fitting them into the existing constitutional laws of Hungary. – *Archduke Stephen, as Governor of Hungary received a letter dated March 17 from Ferdinand V, directing him to implement the content in Kossuth's Manifesto by the Independent Ministerium he appointed.*

3.18   After finishing their work in Pozsony, the members of the diet returned to Pest. On March 23, 1848, **President Batthyány presented his cabinet to the lower house.** *The new Diet* led by Kossuth, now *met regularly in the capital.* Deák, Szemere, Klauzál, Széchenyi etc. working day and night *more than 30 bills were created.* The most *important was the 1848 public law III, which declared, that the executive power of the king can be discharged only through the Independent Hungarian Ministerium.* – It appeared that the reformers were able to receive the elements of a national constitutional government, its leaders working feverishly to make up for the losses the nation suffered since Mohács in 1526.

3.19   True to the *"Divide et impera"* motto of the Habsburg dynasty, the Vienna court started to **intrigue with the territory's minorities** who had been living in relative peace. While the minority delegates on the Pozsony diet were advocating the reforms, the *Kamarilla sent out agents to agitate against Hungarians in public places* among the lower classes. *Upon dynastic instigation, they suddenly proclaimed their desire for independent territories to be carved out from the Hungarian realm.*

3.20   **In Pest** in early April **slogans** appeared on billboards, such as "bread for the people" spreading threatening **rumors.** Lowly groups demonstrated also in front of the National Museum. Nyáry told the crowd not to believe the rumors. Upon the appearance of the Natioal Guard, the *proletarian crowd dispersed.* – A few days later in the taverns *agitators spoke against the Jews.* Many of them were ready to shed some of their customs to fit into the Hungarian society. The Jewish youth organized a national guard troop to show their solidarity, but the regime felt compelled to exempt them from military service as many non–Jews were not willing to work with them.

3.21   While *Croatia was an integral part of the Hungarian kingdom* (partes adnexae); she had many laws of her own choosing and actually *often sided with Hungary* in Hungarian relations with Austria. For example in 1790 they took Hungarian governorship instead of the Austrian. In the reform atmosphere of the period *the Croatians wished to form* **Illyria,** a Southern Slavic country within the Habsburg domain. Their *leader, Lajos Gaj was in direct contact with the Kamarilla.* On March 25 helped by Austrian baron Kulmer, he organized a public meeting in Zagreb, where Jellasics, appointed a day earlier, was celebrated as Croatia's new Governor. Similar to the Pest Resolutions they formulated a **Manifesto**, that included a separation from Hungary. It was carried to Vienna by Gaj himself. The ministry in Pest reacted guardedly; the Hungarian king could not approve a separation. The "law and order" committee of Pest addressed the Croatian separatists with good will.

3.22   The **Greater Serbia** aspiration was to carve out Voivodina from the Hungarian realm. Upon Habsburg instigation in 1790 the Voivodina Serbs petitioned king Leopold II, that *Bács county and the Temes border territory should be governed by a Serbian governor*, a despot. The Kamarilla renewed this affair by agitating strongly for these aspirations. In the middle of March in Újvidék delegates of Serbian and other orthodox communites formulated in *XVI points a petition* addressed to the Hungarian Diet. The petition was carried to Pozsony by Sztratimirivics György and Kosztics Sándor. They threatened Kossuth, that they will bring the petition to Vienna, if rejected by the Hungarian Diet. – In the Temes territory the wild *agitation by the orthodox clergy led to demonstrations* in Nagykikinda, Óbecse, Petrovszello, Mohol, Szent–Tamás, Versecz, Kulpin, Elemér etc. They all started with the destruction of the birthregisters at the churches, that had to be kept since 1840 in the Hungarian language.

3.23   On April 24 in the **riot in Nagykikinda** after they run out of ammunition, two members of the local militia were killed. The crowd freely rampaged with scythes and axes; officials fled except for the two Serbian council members, Izákovics and Csuncsics. *In the blind hate and rage they killed also the Serbian council members in lowly bodily tortures.* Kiss Ernő, commander of the 10th Hussar regiment of the nearby Újpécs had to reconstitute law and order. Revenging Serbs ravaged and burned down his rich mansion in Elemér.

3.24   In **Óbecse** on April 26 *a past delegate to the diet, Zákó István was attacked; the crowd wanted to impale him, because he talked Hungarian in the council*. The crowd rampaged his house; he barely survived an axwound on his head. – The center of the agitation was on Karlóca. **Archbishop Rajasics József** issued a pastoral letter attacking the Hungarian ministerium. He wrote to his Serbian readers to convene on May 13 instead of the 27 as authorized by Csernovics Péter of the Temes Council. To the May 13 Karlóca meeting came also fom nearby Serbia some 600 rugged characters, the serviani, with guns and daggers in their belts. – Rajasics opened the meeting. Gruics and Katyánszky further aroused hatred against Hungarians, who took away the privileges they received from emperor Leopold etc. *The crowd wanted their patriarch and despot.* **Rajasics** was offered and accepted the patriarch status and upon his suggestion a voivod/despot, Supplikácz was elected. The

Kamarilla obliged; promoted colonel Supplikácz to general and released him from his duties in Italy. *Gruics formulated a 9 point Manifesto and Katyánszki made the people swear to fight till they receive a Serbian Voivodina.*

3.25   Among the Slovaks, not really bent on rebellion, the Kamarilla used the Pan–Slavic idea of transforming the monarchy incorporating a large Slavic empire under Habsburg tutelage. As an anti–German movement, the idea had some support by Kolowrat, a member of the Kamarilla. The Slovaks were also invited to the May 31 Pan–Slavic meeting in Prague, but in the ensuing activities by the Kamarilla's secret agents the people did not listen much. But Lutheran ministers, like *Hurban, Stur and Hodzsa* were able to build a follower group. **Myroslav Hurban,** 1817–1890, Lutheran minister in Hlobuka, was in direct contact with Jellasics and with the Prague Pan–Slavic committee; he had some contact also in Russia. When the idea of Pan–Slavism did not excite the populace, frightening, that the Hungarians would liquidate the Slovaks, their children would be kidnapped etc, did. Such rumors were even printed in teacher Stur's Tatranski Orol. On **May 10 in their Liptó–Szent–Miklós meeting** *it was decided, that the Slovaks will organize a voluntary militia to help the Austrian regime maintain law and order.* Stur said, that the time had come to take back from the Hungarians the land, that the Hungarians had taken from the Slovaks. Hodzsa maintained that this is the time to avenge the atrocities of the Hungarians. *The Slovak National Council issued its 4 points Order not to comply with the rules of the Pest government.*

3.26   *To line up the Romanians the Kamarilla used the sensitive issue of the* **"Union with Transylvania"**. – Transylvania was torn away from the Hungarian kingdom by Szapolyai in 1538. Its leaders were willing to accept Turkish "protection" rather than the *Habsburg* rule. Its *despotism* took over in Transylvania and starting from the time the Turks were driven from the territory, *weighed more and more heavily on its people.* Convenient to Vienna burocrats, Transylvania was governed separately from Hungary in spite of the 1790 efforts of the diet confirming its right to be governed by Hungary, being part of her crown. But this was only on paper and was kept disregarded up till 1848, when the *Union with Transylvania* became the 12th point of the Pest Resolution and *was part of Kossuth's Manifesto*, that on March 15, 1848 was *sanctioned by king Ferdinand V.*

3.27   Following their past practice, when the dynasty wanted to have something done for their favor in Transylvania, they turned to the Saxons, who were jealous of their privileges. Notified by the *Kamarilla agents* Salmen, Bruchenthal and Ranicher *started to excite the Romanians promising their help, as in the past, against Transylvania's union with Hungary. – Russian agents told the people about reconstructing the glorious Dacia by uniting Moldva, Transylvania and Wallachia offering a Russian archduke for its king.* Finally Greek orthodox bishop, **Saguna András** took the side of the inciting agents. He was able to make the masses believe, that the tithe, taxes/contributions to be paid by the poor, will not be abolished, it will be worse than before, that the emperor himself wants to liquidate the Hungarians and that the lands of the Hungarian and Seculi upper classes will be distributed among them. On **May 15, 1848** Saguna called a religious meeting in **Balázsfalva,** where the "popas" gathered a mass of 15,000 to 40,000 (as estimated in different resources) Romanian believers. Romanian leaders and agitators were also there: educator *Laureani Trebonius, council clerk Pap Sándor, Timotei Ciparniu, local professor Barnucz Simon and the Greek Catholic bishop Lemény János, the last restraining somewhat the passions. Guerilla leaders, Janku Abraham and Joan Axente*, who caused later much bloodshed, were also present. – The day started with prayer, religious ceremony. From the same pulpit *Barnucz was telling to the throng, that the Hungarians are usurping their land sanctified by Romanian blood, reviled the upper classes, who are exploiting the Romanian people and praised the Austrian emperor*, to whom they can only thank for all. In a closed meeting the day before, lawyers, the Romanian clergy and landowneres formulated a 16 point Manifesto of the people's wish. The people convened in the middle of a green meadow arranged in a dramatic star formation with a pulpit in the center decorated with Austrian and Russian flags. From the pulpit Barnucz read the Manifesto asking the crowd; "do you accept it?" and the throng thundered back: "Yes; we accept it." Then *Saguna blessed the crowd and made them swear allegiance to Ferdinand V*. The Balázsfalva Manifesto was delivered to the king by a 40 member delegation. – On March 17 the leaders formed the 6 member "Romanian National (Pacifying) Committee". Its members provided the imagined structure of Dacia, that Janku was ready to bring into reality. His power was based on the large number of Romanian mountain herdsmen ready to plunder and kill, and on the clandestine help he received from the agents of the Kamarilla. Kossuth's unsuccessful attempt to pacify the Romanians made the pillaging worse. It led to the destruction of Abrudbánya and to bloodier raids on the Hungarian army. In one of its squirmishes Vasvári Pál, a leader of the March 15, Pest Revolution lost his life. – Janku attempted to meet Francis Joseph in Marosvásárhely, when the king in 1852 was touring his Habsburg domain. Governor Ludwig Wohlgemuth did not allow Janku, a leader of "plundering bands" into the presence of a king.

3.28   The Kamarilla tried to *immobilize the reformers also by* **financial machination.** Kossuth had to avert the payment of Austrian State debt. He seized the metal and salt stock of the mines; struck Hungarian coins, printed money and for gold and silver he made the treasury issue promissory notes. See pages 42–44.

3.29   Then on March 27 an ordinance came, that **Ferdinand V revoked his March 15 signature** on the Kossuth Manifesto and on the Idependent Ministerium. The Diet called to his attention to the sanctity of a king's words. Otherwise he would be considered the enemy of the nation. Then scared by the Prague and Lemberg riots *the dynasty decided to sanction publicly the new laws*. At the Pozsony festivities on April 11 Ferdinand V, Charles Francis and Francis Joseph all spoke a few words in Hugarian, except archduchess Sophia, who spoke in good Latin.

3.30   The country was seething by Croatian, Serbian, Romanian and Slovak armed, insurgents. The small security militia at places could not keep order. Rioters ravaged the

Hungarians and their new governmental officials. Secretly the commanders of the well equipped army took their orders from the Kamarilla. *But the parliament still remained constitutionally oriented.* – When the delegation in Vienna to raise a national army did not succeed nor did the attempt to stop Jellasics at the border, it became evident, that the dynasty was unable to maintain balance in the contradictory requirements of the Austrian emperor and the Hungarian king . *The Kamarilla decided to make war on Hungary.* – Batthyány resigned and Deák stepped out of the cabinet, but kept his deputy status. – Kossuth acting as the minister of finance, established a six member **Defense Committee**: Kossuth, Nyáry, Sembery, Madarász, Pálfy and Patay *to govern the country* and to raise a National Army by enlisting volunteers. Kossuth in his paper informed his readers in delicate detail about public affairs.

3.31   In the middle of June about 40,000 Croatian, 30,000 Serbian, over 60,000 border regiments and about 30–40,000 other milita and roving armed bands were ready to carve up the country and completely eradicate Hungary, – *Kossuth was working hard to raise a territorial army* to face the enemy. On July 5, **the first "diet of popular representation"** was called in Pest by the Palatine. Here on July 11, Kossuth sick and exhausted from his hard work, helped by friends, *delivered his most famous address*. Explaining in detail the huge danger the country faced practically abandoned by other nations, *he asked the Diet to grant a 200,000 troop national defense program,* costing yearly 42 million forints; the first 40,000 troop costing 8 to 10 millions. In the dramatic session involving Nyáry Pál, who enthusiastically voted the first "yes," the Diet granted the request. *To foot the bills, he asked the* **citizens to donate their gold and silver**. He successfully has collected the first 12 million forints. *Based on this fund, the first Hungarian paper money was issued.* – By a single oration of Kossuth *the parliament voted to create the* **Hungarian National Army** *and an independent* **Hungarian National Bank.**

3.32   Kossuth's personal magnetism and his unparalleled oratory and leadership mobilized the country. He succeeded *in organizing the new Hungarian military force*, which was aided by contingents of Slovaks and Ruthenians, (later even Hungarian women and guerillas). *To head such a force, following historical traditions, the parliament sent a committee led by Kossuth to Buda asking* **the Palatine,** archduke Stephen *for his acceptance*. Referring to an oath promised to his father, that he would always follow the dynasty's traditional rules, he **refused to be Commander–in–chief.** – But, he went with General Móga to Siófok to meet Jellasics to avert him from military action. He failed, but *he learned, that Jellasics took his instructions straight from the Burg in Vienna and his financial supports from the Austrian Finance Ministerium. Then Archduke Stephen went to Vienna to resign never to return to Hungary.*

3.33   The Chancery appointed Lieutenant General Ferenc Lambert as *commander–in–chief for all the imperial army* against Hungary. When on September 28 he drove over the chain bridge to Pest to dissolve the parliament, his cannons in the castle of Buda pointing to Pest, *the furious* mob recognized him; pulled him from the coach and *beat him to death*. The convening parliament started and investigation to find the culprits.

3.34   On September 29 Jellasics with 24,000 men and 36 cannons met General Móga with 10,000 men and 36 cannons **at Pákozd. The Croatians lost the battle.** Jellasics with few men barely made it to Győr leaving his fellow generals Roth and Phillipovics uncovered. On October 7 at Ozora they were captured together with their troops by General Perczel. – See page 45. Joining with other imperial troops *Jellasics* took control of unstable Vienna and *was appointed the Conmmander–in–chief of all imperial forces.*

3.35   By the end of 1848 the Vienna government had succeeded in putting down the riots and revolutons in the empire with the exception of Hungary. **Ferdinand V**, who had sanctioned the Hungarian Diet's March–April Laws and whose coronation oath obliged him to recognize the substantial measures of independence Hungary had achieved, went against Habsburg self–interest. Thus **the dynasty forced him to abdicate in favor of his nephew, Francis Joseph,** while archduke Charles Francis was waiving his family right for successorship. The new monarch declared in his "Verkündigung", that *his first task was to put down the "rebels" and to fuse his subjects into a single empire.* The new emperor and his government did not consider themselves bound by the previous agreements in Hungary. – Some, like Batthyány, Deák and Wesselényi still hoped for improvment, but the relation increased the despair of the populace. *Kossuth in his newspaper called the change on the throne scandalous. We have the mother of an underage youth telling her son, what to say and he does, what his mother tells him to do.* – This Habsburg policy was confirmed on March 4, 1849, when *the Imperial Court* issued a new constitution annulling the Diet's 1848 April laws and ended Hungary's "de jure" movement for independence.

3.36   The fortune of war favored the imperial army. *Windischgrätz* on January 5 *occupied Budapest. The parliament on January 1, 1849 moved to Debrecen.* Urged by *Batthyány* once more, a delegation was sent to the king to settle his conflict with the nation. At first on January 4th they went to Bicske, where they were rudely refused by the commander–in–chief. *The king would not receive them, because he wants an unconditional surrender.* Windischgrätz kept the delegation captive for five days.

3.37   On February 26 at **Kápolna a major battle** was fought between Windischgrätz's 24,000 men and 147 cannons against Dembinszky's 24,000 men and 105 cannons; both sides claimed victory. *Windischgrätz's boasting report to Vienna,* that he defeated the rebel hordes and will be soon in Debrecen, could have been *responsible for the* **"Kremsier Constitution Document"** of March 14, in which *Hungary* was stripped of Transylvania, Croatia, Voivodina and Fiume and was *absorbed into the empire as a secondary territory.* – In the Upper Danube, Northern, Southern and Transylvanian campaigns *the fortune of war appeared to turn to Hungary's side.* – On January 30 at Szelindek in Transylvania, Bem beat Puchner. Damjanich on March 5 at Szolnok beat Karger. Perczel scattered the Serbs in several battles and on April 3 took from Bosnics their center, Szent–Tamás. On March 27 at the Vöröstorony Pass Bem beat again Puchner driving back to Wallachia the Russian troops, who came to aid the Saxons. On March 19 Bem occupied Brassó forcing the Saxons to surrender. – The troops of Görgei, Damjanics, Aulich, Klapka and Gáspár drove the imperial forces in several battles toward the capital. In a major engagment at *Isaszeg on April 6 the troops of Windischgrätz, Jellasics and Schlick lost the battle.* On April 10 at Vácz Görgei beat General Götz, who fell in the battle. Görgei buried him in full military pomp. To stem the Hungarian military success, the king replaced the Commander-in-Chief Windischgrätz with Welden.

3.38   On *April 14, 1849* meeting of **the Diet in Debrecen,** Kossuth assessed the situation between the dynasty and the nation. He called attention to the many causes of its regrettable condition, such as: – the historiacl events of armed suppression in the last 300 years. – the vicious machinations of the government to drag the nation into a defensive civil war, – the treachery of illegal succession, – the bloody persecutions by minorities instigated by the imperial generals etc. In five points he **called for the dethronement of the Habsburg–Lotharingen dynasty** for the inclusion of Hungary to the independent countries of Europe, a status Hungary had enjoyed previously. *His proposal was cheerfully accepted. The parliament declared him the* **Governing President of the Hungarian Republic.** – The Hungarian decralation of independence was influenced by the American example. Its governor–president was asked to render an account on his action to the parliament. – While this April 14 event was an answer of the December 2 coup d'état and the March 4 Kremsier attempt, it will be the duty of historians to sort out the pros and cons of the crucial dethronement step and its consequences. – *Hungary was the last bastion of the democratic revolutions of 1848, which stood up against the forces of absolutism.* The Hungarian developments were carefully followed with considerable sympathy by the governments and people of Europe and the United States.

3.39   On *May 2 Kossuth appointed the Ministerium of the Republic.* The members of the Cabinet made their decisions independently, except in the question of war and peace, that remained with the Diet. Many different "political solutions" were privately discussed. Kossuth had solid support fortified by the successful military campaign. See page 46. – On April 19 in Óbecse, Perczel beat the Serbs again (see page 47), and on the same day Klapka and Damjanich in a major battle beat Wohlgemut at Nagysalló. On April 20, at Kéménd Gáspár beat Wyss. On April 22, Görgei opened the blockade and put Klapka into the castle of Komárom. – *Kossuth wanted to drive the withdrawing imperial army out of Hungary. Görgei first chose to free Budapest.* – Pest was vacated, but 2,000 mercenaries were left in the "fortress" of *Buda* commanded by General Hentzi, a naturalized Austrian, born in Switzerland. At Pétervárad he was fighting on the Hungarian side, but on January 5, when the imperial army occupied Budapest, he offered his services to Windischgrätz. He fortified the castle. The Hungarian forces were not equipped for taking castles. **Görgei** spent seventeen days, from May 4 to May 21, **taking the Castle.** *It was an expensive victory:* 1022 dead and wounded on the Hungarian side; 1125 dead and wounded on the Austrian side. There were 2284 captives on the Austrian side.

3.40   On May 22 the Kamarilla sent **Francis Joseph to Warsaw** *to ask for military help Czar Nicholas. In return he offered a free hand in the sensitive political issue of the "Oriental Question" dealing with the Russian control of the Bosporus.* On June 14, 1849, more than

200,000 **Russians invaded Hungary** from the north. Meanwhile, the Austrian army was movig against Hungary from the West. On June 18, Cossack troops of General Paskievics inundated Upper Hungary. At the same time, the imperial government in Vienna continued to stir up discontent among the Croats, Serbs and Romanians. The Hungarian army put up a vigorous resistance against the overwhelming enemy forces.

3.41   In early June Hungary's army had less than 160,000 exhausted men against the enemy's overwhelming force: over 250,000 Russians and over 200,000 men in the imperial troops, many of whom were part of Radetzky's victorious army in Italy. The enemy had 1270 cannons and also the territorial militiamen of the minorities. – Realizing the desperate situation, **Kossuth mobilized whatever resources could possibly be found.** His minister of religious affairs, directed the Christian churches to hold country wide fasting and prayers. Kossuth asked English foreign minister Lord Palmerston to intervene in favor of Hungary. Kossuth asked the French not to tolerate the despotism, that Frenchmen had, to attain their Republic. The foreign newspapers all published Kossuth's appeals. The diplomatic efforts of Andrássy Gyula in Istambul, Teleki László in Paris and Pulszky Ferenc in London were fruitless. **Hungary was abandoned by the West.**

3.42   *Managing the Hungarian army* was rather complicated. Part of the problem was, the *polyglot character* of the army in using several languages, and part of it was the individualistic character of *the generals*. – See pages 48–49. – Most of them *were typical, perky soldiers of the period*. They knew about orders and discipline, but little about the *civilian direction, entirely new in the age*. Kossuth had to face the problem of ambition and interpersonal competition. *Particularly difficult was his attempt to handle his able strategist, Görgey,* who did not like foreigners, like Vetter, Dembinszky, and for that matter anybody, whose opinion was different from his. – Kossuth once risked bringing up the subject of the "governor's personal safety". Görgey proudly reassured him. Demonstrating his concern he spent a night personally guarding the "Governor" in front of his bedroom.

3.43   Many battles were lost against the two imperial armies: on June 16, at Zsigárd, on June 20, at Pered, on June 28, at Győr, on July 10, at Beszterce, on July 23, at Szászregen, on July 30, at Segesvár, where "poet laurate" Petőfi died etc. On August 9, at Temesvár Generals Bem and Dembinszky lost a decisive battle against Generals Haynau and Panutine's overwhelming forces. – **Kossuth assigned the leadership to Görgei Arthur** (see pages 50-52). Asked him to negotiate with the enemy (see pages 53–58), but **on August 13 at Arad General Görgei laid down his arms in front of the Russian general, Rüdiger,** expressing that he was defeated not by the Austrians, but the Russians. – By that time, the Russian army was exhausted in the 55 engagements of their Hungarian campaign, 10 of which they had lost. The army was also decimated by sickness and was about to get out of the country. – By early September the remaining 40,000 Hungarian men were defeated in minor battles and the castles held by Hungarians were surrendered except for Komárom. On October 1, Klapka opened the castle to the Austrian Commander–in–chief, Julius Haynau. – See page 59.

3.44   Despite the promises of clemency by the Russian commander and the demands of the English and French governments, **the surrender was followed by a savage reprisal,** by Haynau, the *"Hyena of Brescia." On October 4, Prime minister Batthyány was shut to death in Budapest and on October 6, thirteen generals were executed in Arad. Aulich, Damjanich, Knézics, Lahner, Leininger, Nagy Sándor, Pöltenberg, Vécsey and Török were hung; Dessewffy, Kiss Ernő, Lázár Vilmos and Schweidel were shot to death.* – On August 17, at Orsova with about 5,000 of his followers, **Kossuth** incognito, as Mr. Adam Smith, **fled to Turkey**. They were interned in Viddin, a camp close to the Hungarian border. Sultan Abdul Meshid, respecting the right of hospitality, resisted the Austrian and Russian demands for Kossuth's extradition. For protection he moved Kossuth and his friends to the safer Kutahijah in Asia Minor.

3.45   **Kossuth's family** was also persecuted. Fearing their safety he made his last will in Viddin. After the adversities of a long escape through Serbia, his wife joined him in Sumla. But his three children in Pozsony were kept in custody by the Austrian police. His daughter was to be placed into a convent; the two sons to be raised in Vienna under Austrian surveillance. Kossuth's mother was interviewed by *Commander–in–chief, Haynau, who subjected her to uncivilized rudeness.* Only by the interference of the English Queen were Kossuth's family members freed. The children joined their parents in Kutahiyah, his mother and three sisters remained in Pozsony.

3.46   *The British, US and other West European governments pressured the Sultan not to extradite Kossuth to his enemies.* When Abdul Meshid discontinued the internment of the Hungarian refugees and the Austrian extradition efforts failed, Kossuth and 36 of his close refugee companions were hung "in effigie". – Upon the invitation of the U.S. Congress on September 7, 1851 Kossuth after two years in Turkey, with family and some friends boarded the U.S. Navy's frigate Mississippi in Smyrna (Ismir) to visit in America.

3.47   *About 5,000 friends and followers,* who fled Hungary with Kossuth suddenly became refugees scattered in Turkey, Italy, France, England and the United States. Next to the loss of their country, home and property, they faced existential problems in the receiving countries. In persuit of food and shelter many assimilated in their new environments. Others, when and where it was possible, still worked for the liberation of Hungary.

3.48   En route to the US *Kossuth stopped in Europe to lecture about Hungary's unsuccessful War of Liberation.* He was received with great interest in Gibraltar, Lisbon and London. *In Marseille,* France, where Louis Napoleon was the president of the 2nd Republic, *the police denied his landing.* Nevertheles, moored in the port, the ship was surrounded by boats of cheereing people wanting to see and hear him. A poor worker swam a mile to see him. – *In England* he landed in Southampton, where he was received by a large crowd. *He avoided Lord Palmerston, who wished to see him. This was the same Palmerston, who a few years before acted in favor of the Habsburgs, when Hungary asked for Western help. In London* he was received by large cheering demonstrations. In front of the City Council, the Lord

Mayor himself greeted him. Kossuth delivered his first major address in the Guildhall using the language of Shakespeare. Birmingham, Manchester receiced him with triumphal arches. *He received a book case filled with all the writings of Shakespeare, bought for 9,215 pence collected by about 10,000 workers.* – After six weeks spent in England on November 11, 1851 he left for the United States. His ship, Humboldt, arrived on December 5th in New York's Staten Island.

4. What happened in the Republic of the United States?

4.1   While in France, the Republics and the monarchies kept alternating, in the Habsburg domain, revolutions were suppressed with guns and machinations. *Among the 1848 European liberal reform movements, only Hungary stood up to fight for its constitutional government in a formal war of independence as did people in the United States.*

4.2   In the early eighteenfifties members of the cognitive elite of the **United States**: lawyers, clergy, journalists, teachers in the centers of learning, political **leaders** etc. *were watching with great interest how things are developing in their republican form of government chosen just a few decades before in their successful revolutionay war.* **People were concerned** with the ups and downs of the Republic in France and **with the only other fledgling Republic in the Western world at the time in Hungary.** They read and discussed the turmoils, riots, demonstrations, the bloodsed and ravages; analyzed their causes, motivations, even if the news were late and sometimes were only rumors spread by the Austrian government. The rumors may have been false, but the refugees arriving to the US shores were real.

4.3   At the end of 1849 **one of the scatterd refugee groups reached the shore of the United States.** President Zachary Taylor in his letter of December 20, 1849 to Count Újházy offered the group "protection and free participation in the benefits of our institutions and our laws". *The US. government assigned open, fertile land to the group in the developing Western territory.* The group established a community named **New–Buda** (Új–Buda) (see page 60) in Decatour County, Iowa, where Újházy became the postmaster. – In 1854 the post office handled 950 letters and 7000 newspapers; a remarkably large number for a town of eight houses. But the settlement never counted more than 100 people. – *In 1952, Governor Hampstead invited Louis Kossuth to visit in the State of Iowa, but he declined in a letter received from him on the 10th of May.* Instead, he suggested to the Governor to form Hungarian associations for the purpose of raising "material aid". – Because of their social background few of the new settlers could fit into America's society of self–made men. They tried their hands on everything including land speculation. Several of them enlisted in the Union Armies of the Civil War; others repatriated after the Austro–Hungarian Compromise in 1867. – G. Pomutz became a judge and was rewarded with a foreign consulship. *The town declined;* in 1880 its post office was transferred to Davis City; the place became a ghost town. In 1991 the continued existence of New Buda Township in Decatour County remained the only monument to the rather utopian dreams of the small group of Hungarian exiles.

4.4   **The Hungarian struggles** in the Habsburg lands were followed with special interest in America, especially after March 15, 1848, when **the Hungarians were able to receive without any bloodshed the constitutional sanctioning of Kossuth's Manifesto and their first Independent Ministerium.** People in the US read with disappointment about the dynasty's machinations to play non–Hungarian subjects against the Hungarians. Thus the defeat of Governor Jellasics's Croatian army in the battle of Pákozd by General Móga's new Hungarian national army was widely cheered in the US.

4.5   One of the concerned leaders in the US was Rev. **Benjamin Franklin Tefft**, D.D. a Methodist Episcopal minister. – In 1842 in Boston he became motivated by Signore Alvanola, an Italian revolutionary and refugee. Tefft heard him saying, that the staunch protestant Hungarians are the political future of Southern Europe, especially if they ever break the despotic Habsburg bondage. – Searching in American and British writings, and especially in newspapers, as a member of the Cincinnati "Friends of Hungary" club, he lectured about Hungarian history and Kossuth. He followed closely the events of Hungarian affairs in the Bánát, Croatia. He read also about battles of the long and bloody war of independence Hungary lost against Austria and Russia. *He became concerned with Kossuth's extradition to Austria from his exile in Turkey.* He became disgusted, when the Austrian hireling papers presented Kossuth as an ambitious demagogue responsible for Europe's troubles: all these, to blunt the sympathies of the free nations of the world paving the road for his extradition from the Porte to an ignominious death. – He was called to lecture before the New England Society in Cincinnati (see page 61), where he talked about Kossuth and Hungary and about getting him released from captivity. He repeated his lecture also before the Springfield Lyceum. On January 10, 1850 *he was invited by William Dennison, member of the Ohio House to address the Ohio General Assembly.*

4.6   **The resolutions of the Ohio General Assembly**:

On January 29, 1850 on the motion of Mr. Lawrence and others the Assembly passed the following resolution: "Resolved, That this meeting earnestly urge upon the President of the United States, and upon Congress, to exercise their utmost power to procure the liberation of Kossuth, his associates and family, at the earliest practicable period: *also* to intercede with the Powers of Europe for the liberation of all Hungarians in captivity in such manner as may be most efficient and speedy, and to provide them an asylum in the United States." On motion of Mr. Burns the following resolution was passed: "Resolved, That a copy of the proceedings of this meting be communicated to the President of the United States and to each of our Senators and Representatives in Congress, with the request that the same be presented to each branch of Congress."

The General Assembly passed another resolution: *"Resolved by the General Assembly of the State of Ohio*, That in our deliberate judgement, the present critical condition of General Louis Kossuth, and of his family, loudly call for the friendly and peaceful interposition of the American people. *Resolved*, That we believe it be the duty and privilege of the Congress of the United States, to send immediately an embassy of peace to the Sultan of Turkey, in one of our national ships, who shall be instructed respectfully and urgently to solicit to the Sublime Porte, the liberation of Kossuth and his fellow captives, in the name of the American people, and to take such other steps as shall be best calculated to secure the removal of the great Hungarian and of his afflicted family, to this country. *Resolved*, That our Representatives in the Congres be requested, and that our Senators be instructed, to bring this subject, as soon as possible, before Congress, and to persue such other measures as shall most certainly and speedily carry out, if possible, the objects set forth in the foregoing resolutions. *And it is further resolved*, That the Governor be requested to forward a copy of the fore going to the President, and to each of our Senators and Representatives in Congress."

On February 9, 1850 the Ohio General Assembly passed a "Resolution Relative to Affording Relief to Kossuth and His Fellow Prisoners". It called for the friendly and peaceful interposition of the American people and for the liberation of Kossuth and his associates from captivity taking them to the United States. – The President of the United States promptly adopted the suggestion of the General Assembly of Ohio, and of its citizens of Springfield and Cincinnati, and made the overtures to Turkey that had been thus recommended. See page 62.

4.7 Because of the false statements about Hungary and to the strange misinterpretation of Hungarian history by certain writers, Rev. **Tefft expanded his lectures into a book "Hungary and Kossuth"** of sufficient detail, that can in a wider perspective comprehensively explain the causes and events of the Hungarian War of Independence. The titles in his book's chapters may reflect *the scope of his labor*: – I. Character and condition of the country. – II. Origin and condition of the people. – III. The religions of Hungary. – IV. Language and literature of the Magyars. – V. The Hungarian Constitution. – VI. External relations of the country. – VII. Attempts to overthrow the Hungarian nationality. – VIII. The Magyars defend their nationality. – IX. The Austrian revolution. – X. The rebellion of the Sclaves. – XI. The Austrian invasion. – XII. The fall of Hungary.

4.8 Authorized by the Congress in a 123 to 54 votes, President Millard Fillmore directed Secretary of State, Daniel Webster to instruct the American Embassy in Turkey to take the necessary measures to free Kossuth.. – **The U.S. warship "Mississippi" received him aboard on September 7, 1851. Kossuth** changed ships in Gibraltar and headed for England. From Britain he sailed for the United States on board of the "Humboldt", arriving at Staten Island on December 5, 1851. He was greeted by 200,000 to 300,000 New Yorkers with military ceremony including 100 gunshots (see page 63). He was invited to the White House; he spoke before the Congress. On February 6, 1852, Kossuth addressed the Ohio Legislature, where he stated the following: *"The spirit of our age is democracy. –* **All**

for the people and all by the people. Nothing about the people without the people. – *That is democracy, and that is the ruling tendency of the spirit of our age".* Eleven years later on November 19, 1863, Abraham Lincoln stated in his famous speech at Gettysburg: *"We hereby highly resolve, that these dead shall not have died in vain; that this nation, under God, shall have new birth of freedom;* and that **government of the people, by the people, for the people, shall not perish from the earth."** – Both quotations can be seen on a commemorative plaque at the City Hall of Columbus, Ohio. – The two great men never met, but they represented similar ideas on democracy and liberty as reflected in these quotations.

4.9   **Kossuth** did not enter the United States as an immigrant, but as an **invited politician**. He expressed his ideas about governmental affairs. His elaboration about the **"principle of intervention",** was ahead of his time. More than 60 years passed before America intervened in European politics. – Kossuth spoke to the American people several hundred times during his tour (see pages 64–66). More than 200 poems, dozens of books, hundreds of pamphlets and innumerable editorials were written about him. – See pages 67–71. – Many societies awarded Kossuth honoray membership. Between February 18 and 26 1852, Kossuth and four associates, Count Gregory Bethlen, Peter A. Nagy, Paul Hajnik, Julius Utasy Strasser, were admitted to the degree of masters by the Masonic Lodge No.133 in Cincinnati. – Cities, **a county in Iowa,** streets and infants were named after him. – Still living in 1902 in Cleveleand there was a gentleman named "Éljen Kossuth Wilcox" (Vive Kossuth Wilcox). – Merchants used his name for advertisments. – Kossuth influenced also fashions such as the "Kosuth hat", that became a symbol of revolution. In Habsburg Italy several persons were shot for wearing Kossuth hats.

4.10   Instigated also by Austrian propaganda, *Kossuth had to face substantial adversary opinions*. Just five years before the Civil War **abolition of slavery** was the main political issue in the parturient US society. The Boston weekly, *The Liberator*, a herald of **the abolitionist** *party* was especially hostile. – See page 72. – It ran all the stories related to the *Fugitive Law* requiring every man in the free–States to aid in the arrest of every colored man *accused* of being a slave; there was a penalty of one thousand dollars and six months imprisonment, in case of refusal to help. For months The Liberator ran degrading editorials and diatribes, (including an article by Frederick Douglass) on Kossuth, that he is helping the case of the slave holders by not including abolition in his program. Meanwhile the other major political group, **supporters of slavery** criticized him, because his Champion of Freedom image strengthened the abolitionists' cause. – In a letter to the editor, 'An Inquirer' wrote (probably F. Douglass): "Would you be so very kind as to inform the public, why the Colored Committee with some 'Material Aid' was not admitted to Kossuth as well as other committees. Your truly. An Inquirer". – In this controversial subject, as a foreigner Kossuth remained "aloof", but constantly expounded human rights. He did not wish to interfere officially with domestic politics, but as a private person he spoke up in political matters. – *Kossuth did not foresee, that first America had to solve the slavery problem before it could venture abroad.* This may account mainly for failing in his mission in America. – Today neither the Abolitionist Movement nor the Young America Movement of the 1850s can be analyzed without considering Louis Kossuth. He was often solicited to discuss slavery. In the period's social and economic developments his analyses were important in shaping public opinion on slavery and related subjects. *While he was attacked by some citizens and louded by others, his analyses were noticed by all.*

4.11 **The goal of Kossuth's trip was to receive recognition of the US Congress and to raise money** (see page 44) *for an army so that he could revive the Hungarian revolution. He also was interested in Hungary's banking and shaping European conflicts, catalyzing for freedom movements* – On January 5, 1852, he appeared on the rostrum of the US Senate, was introduced and shook hands with the senators. On a the January 7 banquet his admirer, Secretary of State, William Webster left him with some hope: "We shall rejoice to see our American model upon the Lower Danube and on the mountains of Hungary..... I limit my aspirations for Hungary, for the present, to that single and simple point. – Hungarian independence, Hungarian self–government, Hungarian control of Hungarian destinies." On the same day Kossuth spoke to the House of Representatives, was enthusiastically received, but its members had little to do with foreign affairs. – On his trip returning to Washington on April 13, Kossuth heard about his case being taken up on the floor of the Senate. – *His efforts to persuade the United States government to intervene in Europe had received no encouragement in Washington. Henry Clay, William Seward and President Fillmore had explained, that the doctrine of non–intervention could not easily be overturned.* – **Failing in his mission on July 14, 1852,** on the liner Africa, as Mr. Adam Smith, **Louis Kossuth left the country** to continue his work in Europe.

4.12 **Kossuth gained** some lustre in the US by *siding with the protestants in conflict with Roman Catholic Austria*, and also by *appealing to immigrants*, arriving at a rate in excess of 300,000 per year. He was invited also by German groups. In Utica, he *lectured in German.* – From among those, *who spoke out publicly against him,* the case of **Orestes Brownson** is an example. – Brownson, one of New England's gifted minds, converted from Unitarianism to Catholicism; the Catholics were eager to see and hear him. – In January 1850 he braved the hisses of his audience in New York by attacking in a public address the European revolutionaries. He denounced Kossuth and Joseph Mazzini as conspirators to overthrow by violence the "legally constituted governments in the civilized world." On February 17, 1852, in Cincinnati *he lectured on the subject of "non intervention"* being the wisest policy, staying clear from foreign entanglements. Then avoiding the name of Kossuth, he declared: *"We have no traitors in this country – but we import traitors from Europe and make heroes of them!"* Hisses and shouts of anger interfered with his presentation, but his audience, mostly Catholics, helped him to stop the pandemonium and finish the lecture. But on February 24, O.M. Mitchel, the president of the arranging commercial society, apologized, that *Brownson had "abused the confidence of the Association by traveling outside the proprieties of the lecture hall, to indulge in an indecorous and wanton personal attack."* Next day, Kossuth also commmented, that Brownson was lecturing with *"astonishing boldness and immense ignorance."* Cincinnati was well pleased with Kossuth's answer to Brownson.

4.13 *Monied interest did not side with Kossuth's cause either*. The bankers and investors were afraid, that he would lure the US to costly and dangerous adventures. The *Austrian propaganda line, that the disturbance in Hungary was a "war of races" etc.* was copied by the anti–Kossuth press in England, among them Lord Palmereston, siding with Austria in 1848–1849. The bishop of Pittsburg, speaking for *the Catholic church in the US,* in spite of Kossuth's strong and repeated protest, *saw in him an enemy*. But in a letter to Kossuth the Protestant Episcopal bishop of Ohio expressed his admiration urging him to take his place as near as possible to the feet of Jesus.

4.14 *Kossuth's unusual character* was forged mainly by his experience; his knowledge in history, law, finance, economics; his command of languages, literature, his eloquence; his liberal views about republican ways and last but not least his committment to fight despotism. This **made him a sympathetic leader in the Western world.** – See his last portrait on page 78. – *In Hungary Kossuth* became and continues to be the *popular symbol for the aspirations of the Hungarian people for independence*. He is celebrated annually across the country. – *He became especially popular in the United States*. The country was still developing its constitutional, republican governmental system and a few participants of the War of Independence were still alive. **Kossuth's struggle for Hungarian independence and especially his visit, left a permanent legacy to the United States**, *and perhaps a role model for democratic leadership*. – See pages 73–77. – His achievements were praised by many US notables. Here are quotes from a few such leaders: – *Henry Wadsworth Longfellow* wrote on April 19, 1852 in a letter to Charles Sumner: " Every day brings a new speech by Kossuth – stirring and eloquent. All New York is ablaze with his words... Wonderful power of oratory." – Again on April 30, 1852, in a letter to O. W. Holmes: "wonderful man! to speak so long and so well in a foreign tongue... We were stuck with his dignity". – On May 11, 1852 *Ralph Waldo Emerson* adressed Kossuth in Concord, MA: "We only see in you the angel of freedom... The people of this town... have been hungry to see the man whose extraordinary eloquence is seconded by... the solidity of his action. ... man of freedom, you are also man of fate... you are elected by God... to your task..." – *Theodore Roosevelt*, when addressing a Hungarian–American meeting in 1889: "If you bring into American life the spirit of the heros of Hungary, you have done your share. There is nothing this country needs more than that there shall be put before its men and its future men – its boys and girls too – the story of such lives as that of Kossuth." – Again on April 2, 1910 in the Hungarian parliament: "There is no more illustrious history, than the history of the Magyar nation... The whole civilized world is indebted to Magyarland for its historic deeds". – *Tomas Edison* on March 15, 1928, in a letter to the unveiling of the Kossuth statue on New York's Riverside Drive: "Recalls that, as a four year old, he saw Kossuth and 'asked' a Kossuth hat from his father". – Senator *Robert Dole* on March 15, 1990 at the dedication of Kossuth's bronze bust in the US Capitol in his characteristic staccato style: "... nearly a century after his death, we remember... Kossuth... and celebrate... the democratic idea, to which he dedicated his life... I believe, that Louis Kossuth ... will be very much at home here. I am proud to be here today... this dedication... for more than a century he has inspired all those dedicated to freedom". – *William Cohen* on July 10, 1997 before the

Hungarian Parliament: "Almost 150 years ago, after Kossuth's brave effort to liberate Hungary was brutally crushed, the United Sates invited him to visit... and gave him a hero's welcome, with 100–gun salute... – The Mayor of New York," – Ambrose Kingsland,– "called Kossuth the champion of human progress and universal freedom."

4.15   **The contemporary opinion and style of writing about Kossuth is characterized by Horace Greeley**'s introduction to Headley's book on Kossuth. It is written in the period's rhetoric abundant in oratorical embellishments. – Horace placed him as a Patriot and Hero with Leonidas, Armenius, Tell, Washington, Kosciusko etc., inseparable from stout–hearted, despot–hating leaders, who fought for the Liberty of their people. – His character stood the ordeals of poverty, of sudden eminence, of courtly temptation, of bondage, of exaltation, of unbound sway, of triumph, of deepest calamity, of exile, of strangers' adulation and of reviving hope,... and he has nobly overcome them all. He may be called to die in a palace or dungeon, in his prime or in decrepitude, amid tears or execrations, but his place in history is already fixed and cannot be changed. – He praised Kossuth, as an advocate, journalist, deputy, finance minister and finally Governor of Hungary for his skilled and educated leadership and eloquence with which he created arms, munitions, money, credit and supply for championing their country' liberation. – When Hungary first formally declared independence, she already proved her ability to maintain it. – When Austria solicited Russia's aid, she admitted her lack of ability and the right to govern a neighboring State, if she ever had it. – Kossuth came here to make the people conscious of the majesty of their national position and of the responsibilities, it involves. – He posed the question why could not America next to the millions spent for indulgence to sumptuouos taste and ostentatious display, spend ten millions of dollars to free Hungary and thereby insure the speedy emancipation of all Europe?

4.16   Traveling and lecturing across the US in early **1852, Kossuth's popularity rose to the crescendo of a mania (Kossuth craze)**. – While traveling acoss the country sermons greeted him as the "Hungarian Washington". – For the ladies in Cleveland, he was the "Saint George of Hungarian Republicanism". – In Cleveland *Mr. Aiken*, pastor of the First Presbyterian Curch, the undisputed spiritual leader of the Western Reserve, declared Kossuth "the friend of humanity". – To the leadership educated in Jeffersonian and Jacksonian democracy, Kossuth spoke not as a stranger, but as a brother from the other side of the Atlantic ...., when he said: ".... You, only you can beat down the execrable opposite principle, by acting as an executive power of the law of nations, according to the necessity of your position", – "A Mighty Republic, destined to become the Executive power of the law of nations, upon which rests the independence of the world from all overwhelming despotism". – But there were also other sources of the Kossuth mania. His secretary's wife, Madame Pulszky noted in her diary, that Cicinnati was "starving for excitement." Many of the tensions of a rapidly changing economic and social structure were relieved in the cheers and demonstrations for Kossuth. – What did it matter, that only a very few could hear his words above the clamoring!? –

4.17   Perhaps **his popularity was expressed best** in the year of 1884 in less laudatory rhetorics, than fashionable in 1852, in a quote from "The History of Kossuth, Hancock and Winnebago Counties." which deals also with the naming of the County: – "COUNTY'S NAME. Kossuth county was named after Louis Kossuth, who has long been known as one of the most famous agitators, orators and patriots. His learning and eloquence had been admired on both sides of the ocean, and his heroic struggles for Hungary's independence has stirred the heart and called forth the sympathy of every lover of freedom." *Beyond admiring Kossuth for his ideas and love for democracy, apparently his popularity could not avoid the attention of the deputies in the third Iowa General Assembly, who on January 15, 1851 voted for Kossuth to name their County.*

5. Bibliography

1. Dedication ceremony of the Statue of Lajos Kossuth. Kossuth County Courthouse, July 13, 2001. Program By "Kossuth on State" 150th Anniversary Committee. 12 pages.

2. Encyclopaedia Britannica, 1971. Printed in the U.S.A. ISBN:0–85229–151–5.

3. Hungary and Kossuth: or an American Exposition of the late Hungarian Revolution. By Rev. B.F. Tefft, D.D. John Ball: Philadelphia, New Orleans 1852; 3rd ed. 378 pages.

4. The Life of Louis Kossuth. Governor of Hungary. By P.C. Headley. Derby & Miller, 1852.

5. Kossuth Lajos élete és működése. Írta: Gracza György. A "Budapest kiadás", Budapest 1893; 232 oldal.

6. Az 1848–49.–iki Magyar Szabadságharcz Története. Írta: Gracza György. Lampel Róbert (Wodianer F. és Fiai) Kiadása. Budapest, 1894. december 1. – 5 Kötet; 2343 oldal.

7. Americans from Hungary. By Emil Lengyel. J.B. Lippincott Co. Philadelphia and New York 1948. The Peoples of America Series. 319 pages.

8. Louis Kossuth, "The Nation's Guest" – A Bibliography on his trip in the United States; December 4, 1851 – July 14, 1852. By Joseph Széplaki, 1976. Bethlen Press, Inc. Ligonier, Pa., U.S.A. 160 pages.

9. Historical Dictionary of Hungary. By Steven Béla Várdy. European Historical Dictionaries, No.18. The Scarecrow Press Inc. Lanha, Md. & London,1997. 811 pages.

10. Reflections on the Revolution in France. By Edmond Burke. London 1790. – Töprengések a francia forradalomról és bizonyoss londoni társaságok ezen eseménynyel kapcsolatos tevékenységéről – Jegyzetek. Atlantisz Kiadó, Budapest 1990. Hungarian translation: Kontler László. 1990. 401 oldal.

11. Szabadságharcos napló "A körültem és velem 1848. és 1849. években történt események" Karsa Ferenc. Sajtó alá rendezte Bona Gábor. Zrinyi Kiadó, Budapest. 1993; 383 oldal.

12. Erdély Története, III. kötet; 180–tól Napjainkig. Köpeczi Béla, Miskolczy Ambrus, Szász Zoltán. Akadémiai Kiadó, Budapest 1986. 752 oldal.

13. Dedication by the Congress of a Bust of Lajos (Louis) Kossuth. Proceedings in the U.S. Capitol Rotunda. March 15, 1990, 4:00 p.m. 101st Congress, 2d Session. House Doc. 101–168. 90 pages.

14. Kossuth asked Iowa to Help Cause. Annals of Iowa. July 1947 – April 1949. On page 56.

15. Kossuth's Family – His Mother. News item from Genoa City, Wisconsin. June 8, 1876.

16. Kossuth's sojourn in North America. Biography of Kossuth Lajos. Iowa clipping. File 2. Biography. Kossuth, Lajos. State Historical Society of Iowa. 1 page.

17. Some Hungarian Patriots in Iowa. The Iowa Journal of History and Politics. The quarterly of the State Historical Society of Iowa. October 1913. pp. 479–487.

18. History of Kossuth, Hancock and Winnebago Counties, Iowa. Union Publishing Company, Springfield, Ill. 1884. On page 242.

19. New Buda: A Colony of Hungarian Fourty–eighters in Iowa. By Béla Vassady. The Annals of Iowa. A Quarterly Journal of History by the State Historical Society of Iowa. Summer 1991. pp. 26–52.

20. Streets and towns named after Louis Kossuth in the U.S.A.: *Streets*: Baltimore, Md.; Bridgeport, Conn.; Bronx, N.Y.; Cleveland, Ohio; Columbus, Ohio; Freemansburg, Pa.; Wharton, N.J.; St. Louis, Missouri. – *Towns:* Kossuth, Indiana; Kossuth, New York; Kossuth, Pennsylvania; Kossuth, Mississippi; Kossuth, Florida. From page 121. Louis Kossuth, "The Nation's Guest". By Joseph Széplaky.

21. Kossuth Before Ohio Legislature. Ohio Archeological and Historical Publications. Vol. 12. pp.114–119.

22. Brownson and Kossuth at Cincinnati. By David Mead. Bulletin of the Historical and Philosophical Society of Ohio. April, 1949. pp. 90–93.

23. Kossuth Comes to Cleveland. By Andor M. Leffler. The Ohio State Archeological and Historical Quarterly. 1947; pp. 242–257.

24. Louis Kossuth in Ohio. By Dr. Ronald K. Huth. Northwest Ohio Quarterly. Summer 1968: pp. 111–117.

25. The Liberator. – A Boston weekly. Vol. 21 and 22. 1851, 1852.

26. National Era. – A Washington, D.C. weekly. Vol. 5 and 6. 1851, 1852.

27. The Romanians – A History. By Wlad Georgescu. Edited by Matei Calinescu. Translated by Bley–Vroman. Ohio State University Press, Columbus, 1991.

28. Transylvania – The Roots of Ethnic Conflict. Edited by John F. Cadzow, Andrew Ludányi and Louis Éltető. The Kent State University Press. Kent, Ohio, 1983.

29. Louis Kossuth, Mason and Apostle of World Democracy. By David Kruger, Grand Secretary General of S.G.I.G. in Virginia. The Scottish Rite Journal. June, 2001; pages 5–8.

30. A study how democratic civics worked for preparing Kossuth's visit to America in 1851–1852. Lecture with transparencies on July 10, 2001 at the Immigration History Research Center of the University of Minnesota. By Rezső Gracza. See item FTR–205 on webpage <www1.minn.net/~graczar.>

5. Illustrations

Portraits of Louis Kossuth 39, 78

Documents from the Hungarian War
of Liberation – 1848–1849 . . . . .40–45, 47–59

Resolution of the Ohio State Assembly – February 9, 1850 62

America receives Kossuth, "The Nation's Guest" 63–67, 76–77

Journalistic, artistic and political responses to Kossuth's lectures 68–72

Statues of Kossuth in the United States . . . . .73–75, front cover

Contemporary maps . . . . .46, 60, 61, back cover

Kossuth Lajos. An American photograph. – From the "Szabadságharcz Története" by Gracza György.

A „közrendi bizottmány" első proklamáclója a közönséghez.
Melléklet: „Az 1848—49-iki magyar szabadságharc története" czimű műhez

Pest város közönsége nevében alolirottak szerencsések hivatalosan értesiteni a' magyar nemzetet, hogy a' mi más országokban polgár vérbe került, — a' reformot — Budapesten 24 óra alatt békés és törvényes uton kivivta a törvényes egyetértés. A városi tanács ugyan is a' választó polgársággal értesülvén arról, mikép a' város polgárai és lakosai vele együtt akarnak értekezni az idők komoly fejleményei felett, a' tanácskozási teremek századokon át zárva volt ajtajit 1848-dik évi martius 15-kén délután 3 órakor a' népnek megnyitá, 's miután megértette annak törvényes kivánatait, azokat mint nagyobb részt már eddigelő is kebelében ápolt hazafiui óhajtásokat, egy szivvel egy akarattal elfogadta magáévá tevé, sőt azon tizenkét pontot, mellyeket nagy részben a' nemzet 1790-dik év óta törvényhozás útján is annyiszor sürgetett; ezen közgyülésben az országgyüléshez intézendő kérelmezéskint aláirta.

A' nemzet óhajtásainak említett pontjai következők:

1. **Sajtó szabadság a' censura eltörlésével.**
2. **Felelős ministerium Buda-Pesten.**
3. **Évenkénti országgyülés Pesten.**
4. **Törvényelőtti egyenlőség polgári és vallási tekintetben.**
5. **Nemzeti őrsereg.**
6. **Közös teherviselés.**
7. **Urbéri visszonyok megszüntetése.**
8. **Esküttszék, képviselet egyenlőség alapján.**
9. **Nemzeti bank.**
10. **A' katonaság esküdjék meg az alkotmányra, magyar katonáinkat ne vigyék külföldre, a' külföldieket vigyék el tőlünk.**
11. **A' Politicai status foglyok szabadon bocsáttassanak.**
12. **Unio Erdélylyel.**

A "Közrendi Bizottmány" első proklamáclója a közönséghez. Költ Pesten 1848dik év martius l5kén. Aláírások: Rottenbiller Leopold választmányi elnök, Klauzál Gábor, Nyáry Pál, Egressy Sámuel, Irinyi József, Staffenberger István, Molnár György, Irányi Dániel, Vasváry Pál, Petőfi Sándor, Tóth Gáspár, Gyurkovics Máté, Kacskovics Lajos. From The "Szabadságharcz Története". By Gracza György.

Következtek a' közgyülés határozatai miszerint a) **Pest város** iménti közkivánatait egy választmány haladéktalanul személyesen terjeszsze elő az ország rendeinek Ő Felségét pedig hódolva szeretett koronás királyunkat kérje meg, hogy ezen országgyülést minél előbb Pestre tegye át. b) A' közgyülés alolirt választmányt bizta meg, hogy a' rend fentartásaul czélszerüen intézkedve, határozatait foganatositsa.

Mellyeknek teljesitéseül alolirt választmány kiküldetéséhez képest.

a) Tüstént átmene Budára a' Nagyméltóságu magyar királyi helytartó tanácshoz, 's ugyanott azon kormányszéki határozatot nyerte, melly szerint a' censura nyomban megszüntettetett, a' sajtó annyi századas bilincsei alól fölszabadult, 's addig is, mig sajtó törvények hozatandnak, a' sajtókihágások felett a' nemzet bizodalmát biró 's a' Nagyméltóságu helytartó tanács által a' hozandó törvényig ideiglenesen kinevezendő egyének fognak a' fenálló törvények szerint. Ime e' lapok is tanusitják a' határozat foganatát.

b) Kieszközöltetett, hogy a' sor-katonaság nem fog a' rend fentartásába elegyedni, mellynek biztositásaul alolirt választmány intézkedett, hogy a' pesti polgári őrsereg eddigi száma jelenleg 1500-ra szaporittassék 's mint nemzeti őrsereg nemzeti szinekkel ékesittessék.

c) Kieszközlötte, hogy Stancsics Mihál hazánkfia, ki azért mert szabadon irt, mint statusfogoly Budán le vala tartóztatva birói itéletig nyomban szabadon bocsáttatott, 's a' nép kiséretében családjának adatott vissza.

Illy békés és törvényes uton minden vérontás és csendzavar nélkül kivivott nagyszerű reform-diadal megünnepléseül holnap Budapest ki leszen világitva, 's innentúl Pest város, mint a' haza szive törvényházának tornyán nemzeti szinű zászló lobogand.

Budapest a' törvény és béke korlátait nem sérté meg, 's miután a' rend fentartása hazafiui érzelmü lakosainak kezébe tétetett, reményli: hogy az egész haza ebben is követni fogja példáját.

Költ Pesten **1848**dik évi martius 15kén.

Rottenbiller Leopold s. k. *Molnár György s. k.*
  választmányi elnök.   *Irányi Dániel s. k.*
Klauzál Gábor s. k.   *Vasváry Pál s. k.*
Nyáry Pál s. k.   *Petőfi Sándor s. k.*
Egressy Samuel s. k.   *Tóth Gáspár s. k.*
Irinyi József s. k.   *Gyurkovics Máté s. k.*
Staffenberger István s. k. *Kacskovics Lajos s. k.*

*The first proclamation of the "Law and Order Committee". The 12 demands of the proclamation: 1. The freedom of the press from censure. 2. Responsible Ministerium in Buda-Pest. 3. Yearly diet in Pest. 4. Civic and religious equality before the law. 5. National defense army. 6. Common sharing in taxation. 7. Abolishing of statute labor. 8. Common jury, representation based on equality. 9. National Bank. 10. The military to take oath on the Constitution; Hungarian soldiers should not serve in foreign lands; foreign soldiers to be called away. 11. The political status prisoners to be released. - 12. Union with Transylvania.

Banknotes of the the Hungarian War of Independence. – From the collection of R. Gracza.

*Note, that on the banknotes printed after the dethronement on April 14 in Debrecen, the crown above the coat of arms was deleted. For back of "Tiz Forint" see next page.

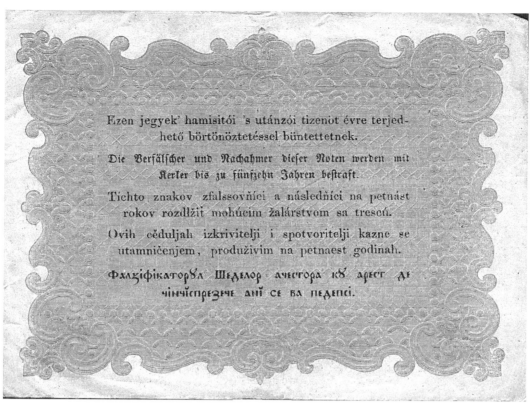

Banknotes of the the Hungarian War of Independence. – From the collection of R. Gracza. (continued)

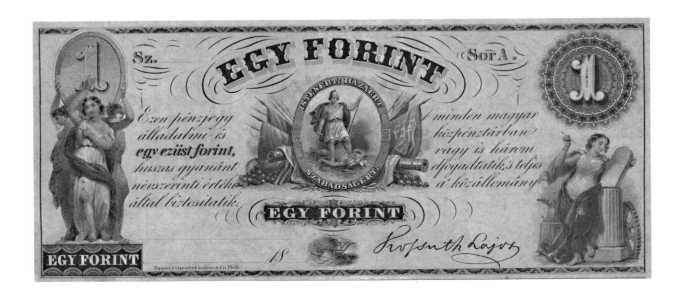

Hungarian banknote and a promissory note printed in the United States to be eventually used after the expected liberation of Hungary planned by Kossuth. – From the collection of R. Gracza.

Kiáltvány a horvát hadsereg lefegyverzéséről.

Melléklet: Gracza György „Az 1848—49. Magyar Szabadságharcz Története" cz. műhöz

ÖRÖM HIR! Freuden Nachricht!

Roth és Philippovics Tábornokok Dandára nincs többé!

Éppen e perczben hozza Perczel Gyula, Tolna Megye Főbírája, mint szemtanú s a kivívott dicső Diadalnak munkás részese, azon hivatalos tudósítást:

Mi szerént, tegnap October 7-én Ozorán, Tolna szélén a Sió mellett, Tolna Megye öszves felkelt Népe, a már csak futásban menekvését kereső Ellenségnek utját állván, az elő csatárok által váltott csak néhány puskalövés után, mellyek közülünk egy embert sem ejtettek el, az öszves sereget fegyvereik letevésére kényszeríték!

Az eredmény ez:

Négy Zászló, Tizenkét Ágyú, Huszonnégy Munitiós szekér, Hat ezer ötszáz Hadi fogoly, közlük Roth s Philippovics Tábornokok, öszves tisztikarokkal, kik közt két Tüzér tiszt nálunk szolgálatot vállalt.

Hazafiak! isten az igazságos ügyet el nem hagyja, hitszegés s árulás más gyümölcsöket nem teremhetnek mint alávaló eszközeiknek a boszuló Nemesis általi lesujtását!

A dölfös Pártütő Jellacsics ki a magyar korona gyöngyei után szemtelenkedett kezeit kinyujtani, kengyelfutóvá lealázva, gyülevész népei mint őszszel a legyek hullanak el! Kevés nap még csak, s bitor Ellenség nem fogja Hazánk szent földét tiporni!

Remény, Csüggedetlenség kebleinkben, az ezredéves magyar vitézség még nem tagadta meg magát, miénk a Győzelem! — mert vélünk van Isten és igazság! — Éljen a Szabadság, Egyenlőség, Testvériség! —

Pécs october 8-án 1848.

Pécsett, nyom. a lyc. nyomdában.

Das Truppen Chor der Generäle Roth und Philippovics ist nicht mehr!

Diesen Augenblick bringt Ober-Stuhlrichter Julius Perczel von Tolna, als Augenzeuge, und thätig Mitwirkender des großen Sieges, die officielle Nachricht:

Daß am 7. October gestern zu Ozora, in Tolnauer Comitat am Flusse Sió, der gesammelte Landsturm desselben Comitats, den Ausweg des schon in wilder Flucht begriffenen Feindes hemmend, nach wenigen gegenseitig gewechselten Plänkler Schüßen, wobei wir keinen einzigen Mann verloren, das ganze feindliche Chor, zur Streckung der Waffen zwangen!

Die Resultate dieses großen Sieges sind:

Vier Fahnen, zwölf Kanonen, vier und zwanzig Munitions-Wägen, sechs Tausend und fünf hundert Gefangene, darunter die Generäle Rott und Philippovics, sammt ihrem ganzen Officiers-Chor, von welchen zwei Artillerie Officiere um unsere Dienste nachsuchten.

Patrioten! Gott verläßt die gerechte Sache nicht! Meineid und Treulosigkeit können keine andere Früchte tragen, als schonungslose Schläge der rächenden Nemsis!

Der hoffärtige Landes Verräther Jellacics welcher sich erdreustete, mit frechen Händen nach der schönen Perle der ungarischen Krone zu greifen, muß beschämt das Metier eines Schnellläufers ergreifen! wenige Tage nur, und kein Meuterischer Feind wird die heilige Scholle unseres Vaterlandes mit Füßen treten!

Darum flamme Hoffnung Unerschütterlichkeit in unsern Busen, die Tausend jährige ungarische Tapferkeit kann sich nie verläugnen, Unser ist der Sieg! denn mit uns ist Gott! die Gerechtigkeit! Es lebe die Freiheit, Gleichheit, Brüderlichkeit! — —

Fünfkirchen den 8. October 1848.

Kiáltvány a horvát hadsereg lefegyverzéséről október 7-én Ozorán. Perczel Gyula, Tolna Megye Főbírájának jelentése. Pécs october 8-án 1848. From the "Szabadságharcz Története". By Gracza György.

*Proclamation about the disarmament of the Croatian Army at Ozora on October 7th (1848).

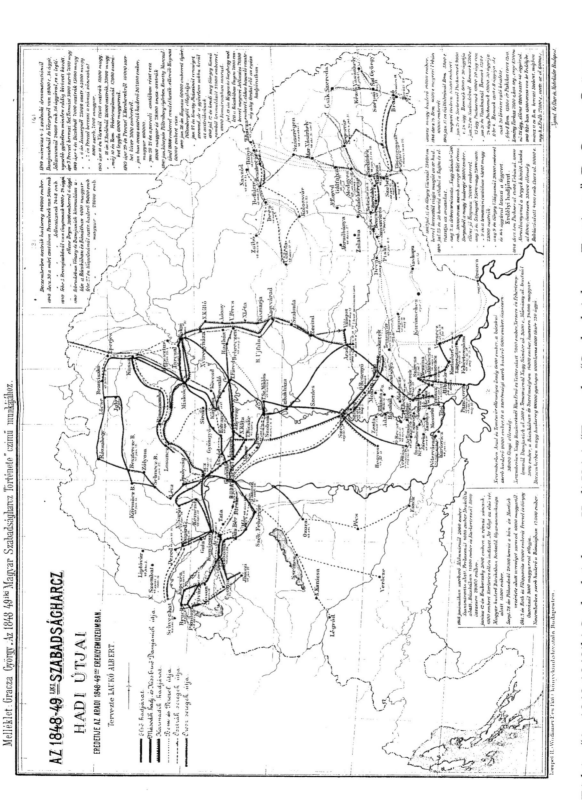

Térkép: "Az 1848-1849iki Szabadságharcz Hadi Utjai. "From the "Szabadságharcz Története". By Gracza György.

*Map: The battle routes of the 1848-1849 War of Independence.

SZENT-TAMÁS BEVÉVE.

PERCZEL

tábornokunk april 3. következő jelentést külde.

Reggeli 8 órától 10 és fél óráig tartott erős ágyuzás után Szent-Tamás végre rohammal vitéz seregem által elfoglaltatott. 4 lobogó, 6 ágyú, tömérdek vagyon és fegyver, lőszer esett birtokunkba. A támadás és rohanás Kis-Kér és a Verbász felöli sánczokra egyszerre történt. Az ellenség, mely elszánt vitézséggel sok ezernyi mennyiségben utolsó perczig tartá magát, s megszámithatlan mennyiségű holtakat veszte, 4—5,000-en tul lehet az elesettek, a vizbe haltak vagy hajtattak száma. Mi is több tisztet és vitézt veszténk, kik dicsően haltak el e dicsőség és eredménydűs ostromban.

Isten segitségével Bács már ismét miénk, és a haza szabaditására—a lázadás első fészkének elfoglalása s elrombolása által—nevezetes lépés történt.

Földváry a szegedi szabad csapat őrnagyja, és csapatja utánna, voltak az elsők, kik a hid fősánczot bevették. Ő a csatapiaczon általam a kis érdemjelre érdemesittetek.

Gál ezredes vezeté a verbászi sánczok elleni támadást, hol a 8- és 50-ik honv. z. aljak, és a Vása gyalogság tüntették ki magokat.

Perczel Miklós alezredes vezénylé a hidfő sáncz megtámadását, melynek bevétele dönté el Szent-Tamás sorsát. E sáncz bevételénél az oldalas rohamot vezető Bach kapitány, a homlokon rohanó Turszky zaszlóalj Rainer őrnagy alatt jeles vitézségöknek elvitázhatlan tanuságát ada.

A tüzérség becsületesen megfelelt hivatásának.

Általában az egész sereg, lovasság, gyalogság egyiránt megtevé kötelességét. Ők tökéletes harczfiak.

Gr. Batthyány Kázmér a jeles és bátor hazafi osztá velem e nagy napnak fáradalmait és veszélyeit.

Debreczen, april 5. 1849.

a honvédelmi bizottmány.

Perczel Mór tábornok jelentése Szent-Tamás bevételéről 1949 március 3-án a Honvédelmi Bizottmánynak. Debreczen, április 5. 1849. From the "Szabadságharcz Története", By Gracza György.

*Report of General Perczel Mór to the National Defense Committee. Debreczen, April 5, 1849.

Kossuth Lajos németnyelvű levele Guyon Richard tábornokhoz. Szeged, 1849 július - Letter of Louis Kossuth written in German to General Richard Guyon; dated on July 16, 1849. From the "Szabadságharcz Története". By Gracza György.

Drága tábornok ur!

Fogadja a haza forró háláját a tizenegyediki dicső fegyvertényeért és az én szivből jövő köszönetem szives értesitéseért.

Nagy bizalommal nézek a hadművelet további eredménye elé, mert egy oly dicső hadsereg, a melynek élén Guyon oroszlán áll, biztos a győzelem.

Különben minden jól van tervezve, be kell vallanom, hogy nekem Titel bevétele olyan fontosnak látszik, hogy azt mondhatnám, ez képezi a végeredmény alapját és mégis azt kell mondanom, hogy a helyzet nehézsége nagyon a szívemen fekszik.

Sokkal biztosabbnak látszik előttem az eredmény, ha Jellasicsot nem Titel után, hanem Titel előtt szorithatnánk a Dunához.

Ott most összpontosítva van és azért nagyon erős. — Bánffy Perlaszról keveset segithet. — Mert neki tizennégy hídon kell keresztül menni és csak akkor van maga előtt a Tisza, a melyen aztán nem mehet keresztül.

Igazán nem tudom, nem volna tanácsosabb, hogy mialatt Bánffy Jellasicsot Perlaszról fenyegeti, ön kedves tábornok ur, Temerin és Csurogról csupán demonstrál és maszkirozza csak a szükséges mozdulatokat, derék hadtestének nagyobb részével pedig éjjeli marssal Ujvidék mellett keresztül hatol a Dunán és egyesül Kmetivel és megerősödik a péterváradi csapattal, hősies küzdelemmel bevéve Kameniczet és Karloviczát, és csak ezután az egyesült sereggel támadn'a meg Jellasicsot.

Beszélje meg ezt Vetter altábornagygyal, akinek kérem tiszteletteljes köszönetem átadni.

Komáromnál tizenkettedikén a felső csapatnak erős ütközete volt. Eredményt egyik fél sem ért el. Nagyon sok a veszteség. Az ellenségnél nagyobb, különösen lovasságban.

A Tiszán túl nincs orosz.

Tokajtól kezdve lefelé az egész vonal a mi kezünkben van.

Perczel 26 ezer emberrel Szolnoknál és Abonynál, Kazinczy nyolcz ezer emberrel vonul Tokaj felé.

Az orosz Kula és Gyöngyöstől áll Pestig és Váczig.

Drága barátságába ajánlom magam, a hazát és a szabadságot pedig nemes szivére és dicső seregére bizom.

Szeged, 1849. jul. 16.

tiszteletteljes szolgája

Kossuth Lajos.

*Richard Guyon, professional soldier was born in Scotland. In 1832 he was serving in the Austrian army in Hungary, where he married a Splényi baroness and retired to attend to their estate. But in 1848 he joined the Hungarian military forces; in taking fort Mannsworth, he distinguished himself. Recognizing his skill Kossuth appointed him to the position of general. Avoiding politics everyone in the Hungarian army respected him. He fled with Kossuth to Turkey, where he settled. As Pasha Kursid he died in 1856 in Constantinople.

Görgei Arthur utolsó levele Kossuth Lajoshoz a világosi fegyverletétel előtt; Arad, 1849 aug. 1. From the "Szabadságharcz Története". By Gracza György.

*The last letter of Arthur Görgei to Louis Kossuth; Arad, on August 1, 1849 before the surrender at Világos.

> Görgei Arthur tábornok,
>
> Kormányzó ur, a minister elnök ur ellenjegyzése mellett, engem az ellenséges haderőkkeli egyezkedésre felhatalmazó levelét kézül vettem, minthogy ezen felhatalmazás azonban a kivánt és közös hazánk jövőjét biztositó cél elérésére nem elégséges, és én arra hogy azt a mit a nemzet számára megmenthető, megmenthessem, elkerülhetetlen szükségesnek tartom, hogy a jelen kormány lépjen le, s én ruháztassam fel a polgári s katonai legfőbb hatalommal, tehát tisztelettel felkérem kormányzó urat méltóztassék ekkép mielébb határozni; ezen határozatát velem, s a Községgel is tudatni,

The last letter of Arthur Görgei to Louis Kossuth (continued)

hogy annak következtében minden késedelem nélkül azon
lépéseket megtehessen, mely-
lyek egyedül képesek a nemzet jövőjét biztosítani, s azt
a megromlástól még nem késő
megmenteni.

Görgei Arthur
tábornok

L Leher efer
hogy

L lag-hiflers

The last letter of Arthur Görgei to Louis Kossuth (continued)

Kossuth Lajos utolso levele Görgeihez augusztus 12kén From the "Szabadságharcz Története". By Gracza György.

*The last letter of Louis Kossuth to Görgei on August 12, 1849.

The last letter of Louis Kossuth to Görgei (continued)

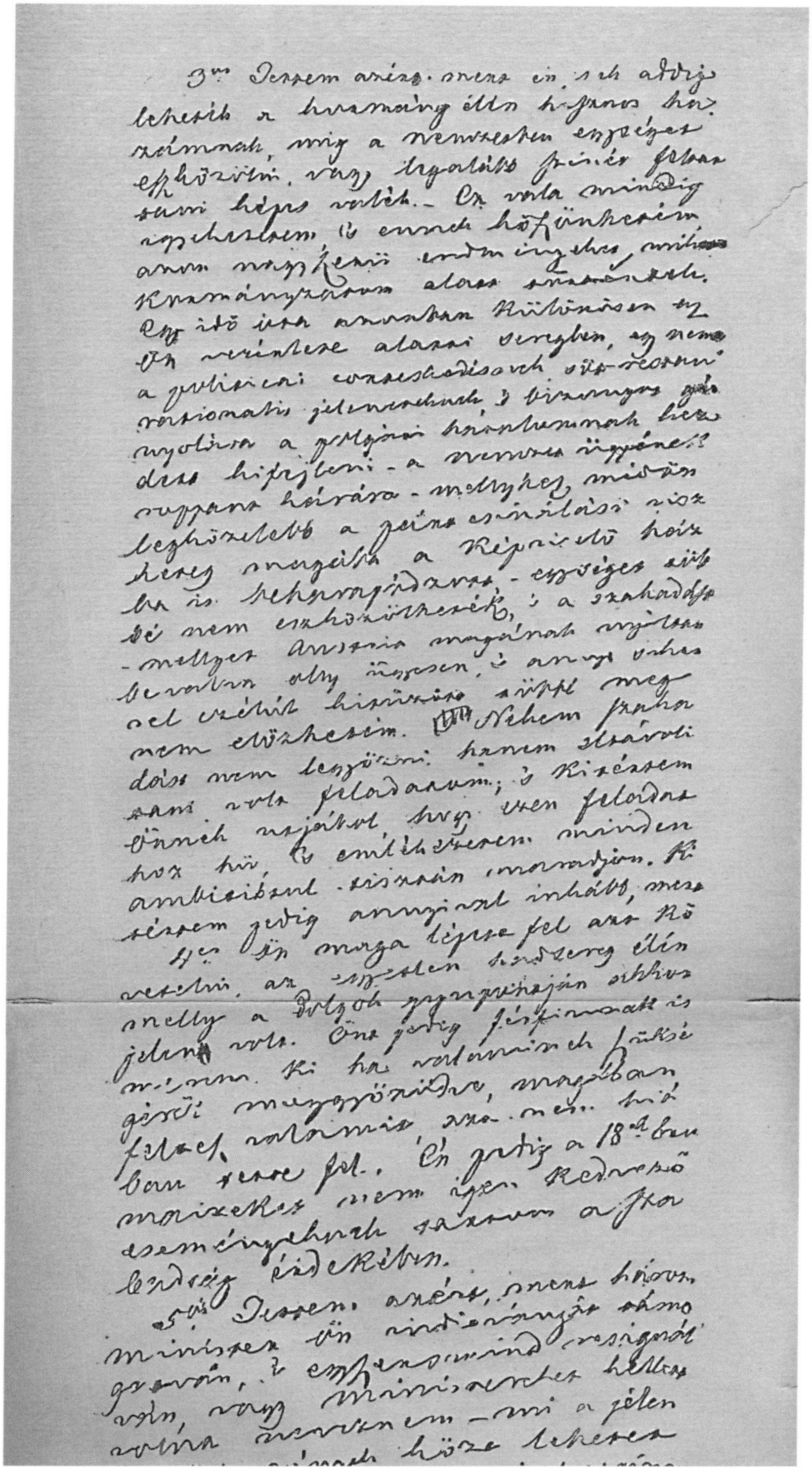

The last letter of Louis Kossuth to Görgei (continued)

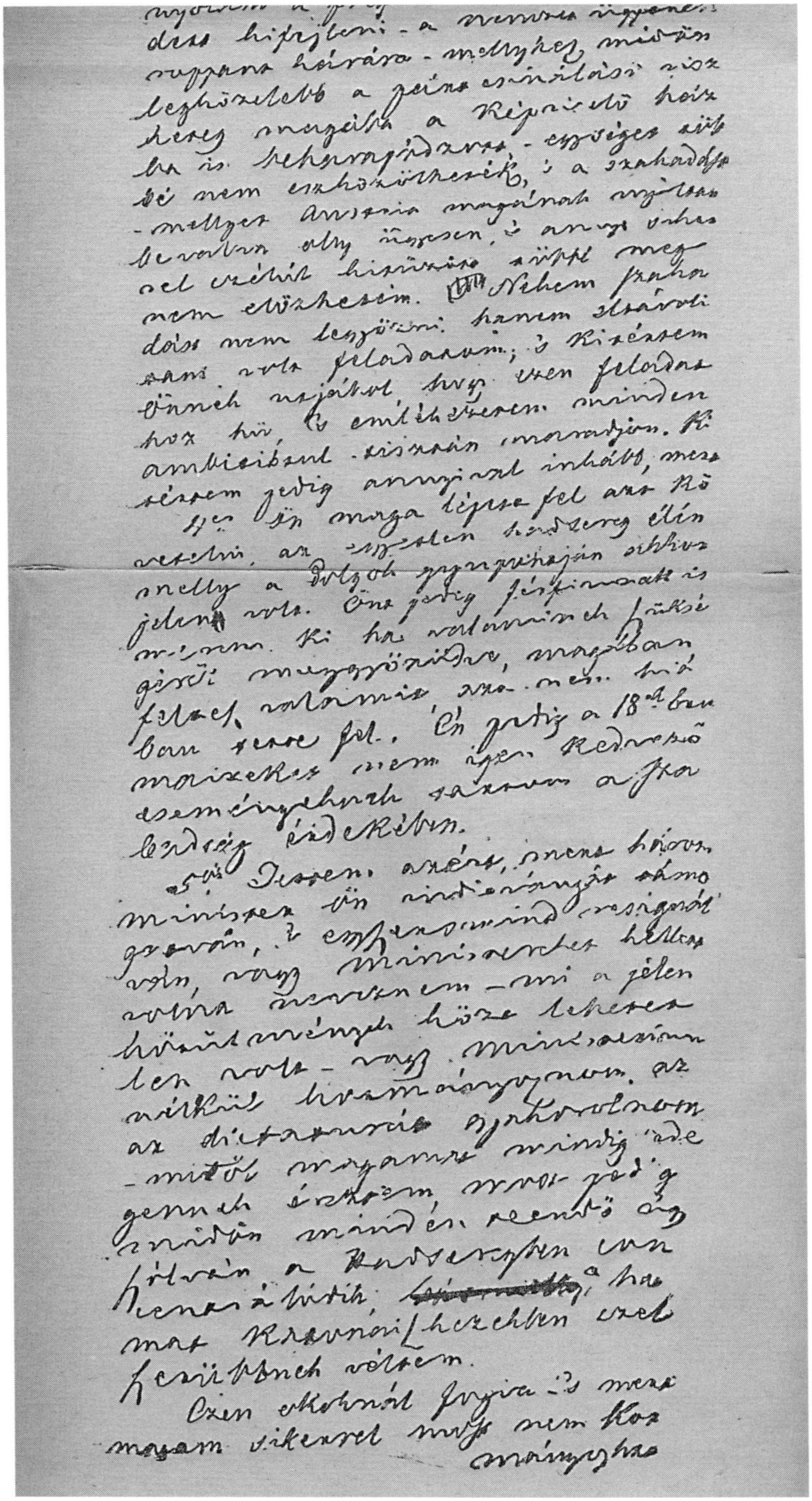

The last letter of Louis Kossuth to Görgei (continued)

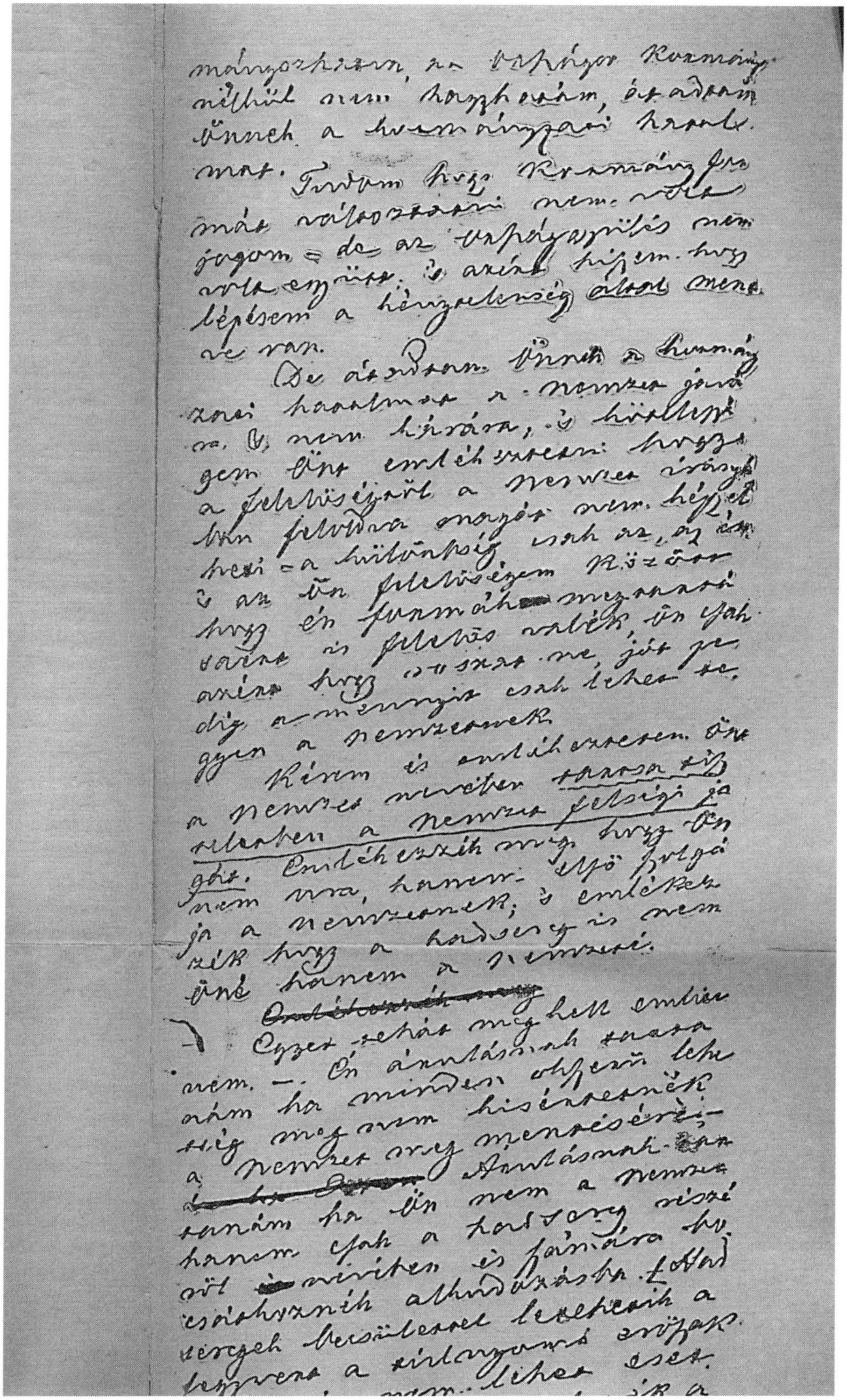

The last letter of Louis Kossuth to Görgei (continued)

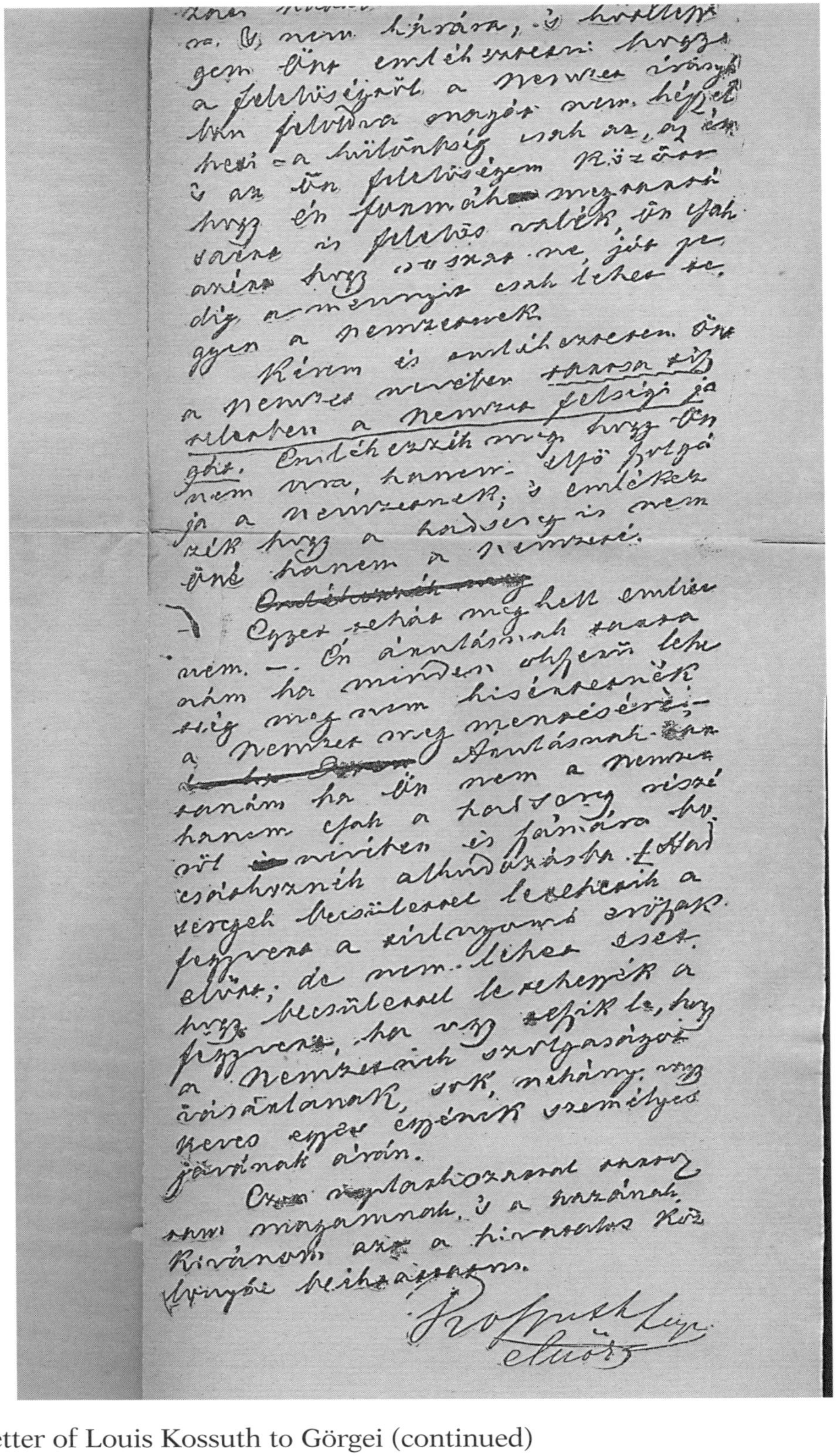

Kossuth Lajos
elnök

The last letter of Louis Kossuth to Görgei (continued)

Klapka György tábornok és Újházy László kormánybiztos "Szózata a feldunai magyar néphez" Komárom elfoglalásáról 1849 augusztus 3-an. From the "Szabadságharcz Története". By Gracza György.

*Proclamation of the Hungarian people of the Upper Danube by General Klapka György and National Commissioner Újházy László about the occupation of Komárom on August 6, 1849.

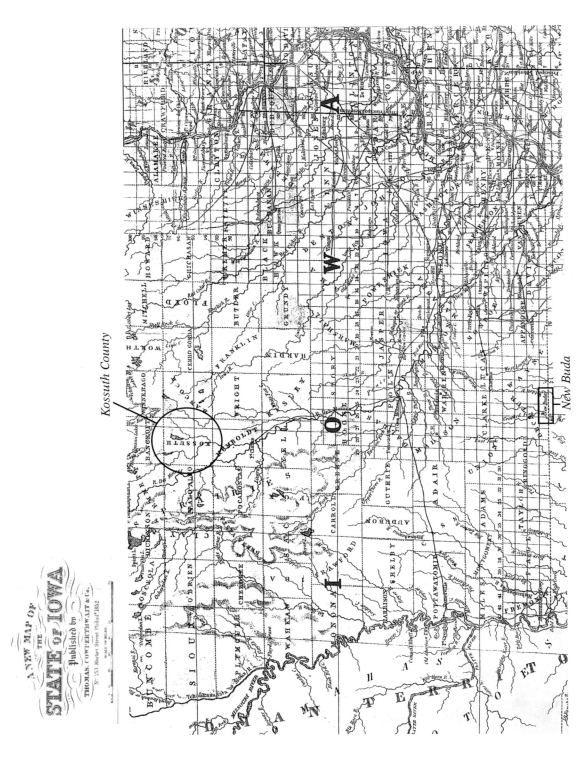

A New Map of the State of Iowa published by Thomas, Cowperthwait & Co. Philadelphia, 1852. – From the Kossuth County Historical Society. Algona, Iowa.

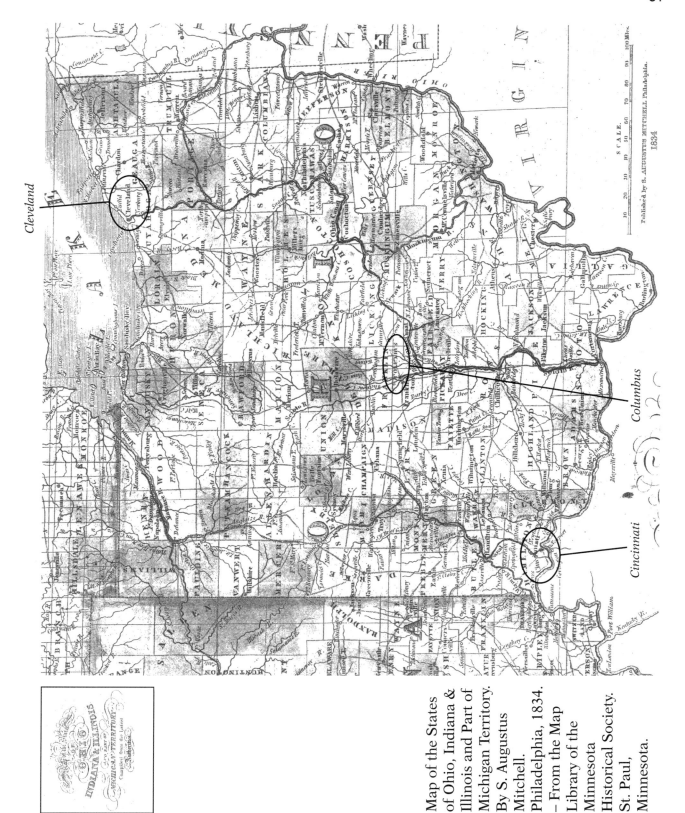

Map of the States of Ohio, Indiana & Illinois and Part of Michigan Territory. By S. Augustus Mitchell. Philadelphia, 1834. – From the Map Library of the Minnesota Historical Society. St. Paul, Minnesota.

RESOLUTIONS
RELATIVE TO AFFORDING RELIEF TO KOSSUTH AND HIS FELLOW PRISONERS.

Whereas, It is well known, that in the years 1848 and 1849, during a general revolution among the nations of Central and Southern Europe, the ancient kingdom of Hungary, for reasons believed to be satisfactory, declared herself to be independent of the Imperial house of Hapsburgh, and of the Austrian Government and Empire. That in maintaining this declaration, this kingdom pursued the most natural justifiable and patriotic measures—that she twice drove her enemies beyond her borders, thereby, according to the law of nations, positively achieving her independence. That subsequently, an army of Russian mercenaries, employed and paid by the Emperor of Russia, invaded the kingdom of Hungary; that the Hungarians, nobly struggling for their lives and liberties against the united forces of two powerful despots, nearly secured their independence the second time, and would undoubtedly have done so, had it not been for a deed of treachery—that this treachery, by which an army of nearly two hundred thousand strong, and about fifteen millions of heroic and determined people were delivered up to their oppressors, was instigated by large and tempting bribes offered by the unscrupulous invaders, and that in this unmanly way, and not by the usual means of warfare, the independence of Hungary was defeated.

Whereas, Furthermore, it is equally well known, that from the beginning to the close of this eventful struggle, the illustrious Louis Kossuth was the leading man of Hungary—that he had devoted all of his precious life to the emancipation, elevation and glory of his country,—that during the progress of the revolution, he threw himself, his property, his family, his friends, his future hopes and prospects, unreservedly and magnanimously into the scale, to secure the freedom of his native land; that contrary to the advice of many of his warmest friends, but prompted by the purest and holiest motives, and in imitation of our own revolutionary forefathers, by his sole authority, and on his own responsibility, he solemnly proclaimed Hungary a Republic; that the almost superhuman exertions made by him to establish a Republican government, and thus guarantee the freedom and happiness of his countrymen, challenge the admiration of all nations, and that in the fall of Hungary, and in his own flight for personal safety, not only has his reputation as a Commander not been tarnished, but his duties as the head of a temporarily unsuccessful, but not yet hopeless effort, have been both maintained and honored.

Whereas, also, it is generally notorious, that at this time the Hungarian Patriot, contrary to the law of nature and of nations, is held in captivity by the Sultan of Turkey, though not a solitary crime against the Turkish government has been alledged against him; that Russia has demanded the delivery of him into her hands, in order to his being punished as a rebel and malefactor; that she is now arming her soldiers for the purpose of sweeping down at the earliest opportunity, to take forcible possession of his person, and that in all human probability, she will get possession of him, and hurry him into her own territory, there to shed his blood by some barbarous method of execution, unless she is anticipated in her movements by the timely interposition of some free and friendly nation.

Whereas, Finally, it appears from our most reliable advices, that the wife, the mother, the children and other members of the great Patriot's family, have been lying for the past three or four months in an Austrian prison, that they have been recently released from confinement, that they are dependent for their daily bread upon the hard charities of Kossuth's enemies, and that while he is kept in utter ignorance of their condition they are allowed to know nothing of the fate that has befallen, nor of the yet sadder fate that awaits him. Therefore, it being the duty of all free people, and of the American people in particular, to extend the hand of sympathy and fellowship to a suffering Patriot and Republican, when unrighteously treated and shamefully abandoned, after having made such great and irrecoverable sacrifices for the cause of human freedom, it is hereby

Resolved by the General Assembly of the State of Ohio, That in our deliberate judgment, the present critical condition of General Louis Kossuth and of his family, loudly calls for the friendly and peaceful interposition of the American people.

Resolved, That we believe it to be the duty and privilege of the Congress of the United States to send immediately an Embassy of Peace to the Sultan of Turkey in one our national ships, who shall be instructed respectfully and urgently to solicit of the Sublime Porte the liberation of Kossuth and his associates in captivity, in the name of the American people, and to take such other steps as shall be best calculated to secure the removal of the great Hungarian and of his afflicted family to this country.

Resolved, That our Representatives in Congress be requested, and that our Senators be instructed, to bring this subject as soon as possible before Congress, and to pursue such other measures as shall most certainly and speedily carry out, if possible, the objects set forth in the foregoing resolutions. And be it further

Resolved, That the Governor be requested to forward a copy of the foregoing resolutions to the President, and to each of our Senators and Representatives in Congress.

BENJAMIN F. LEITER,
Speaker of the House of Representatives.
CHARLES C. CONVERS,
Speaker of the Senate.

February 9, 1850.

Resolution Relative To Affording Relief To Kossuth and His Fellow Prisoners. By the Ohio State Assembly, February 9, 1850. From the Ohio Historical Society. Archives, Library Division. Columbus, Ohio

Contemporary Lithograph of Louis Kossuth's reception in New York City on December 6, 1851. – From "Dedication of Kossuth's bust". House Doc. 101–1680.

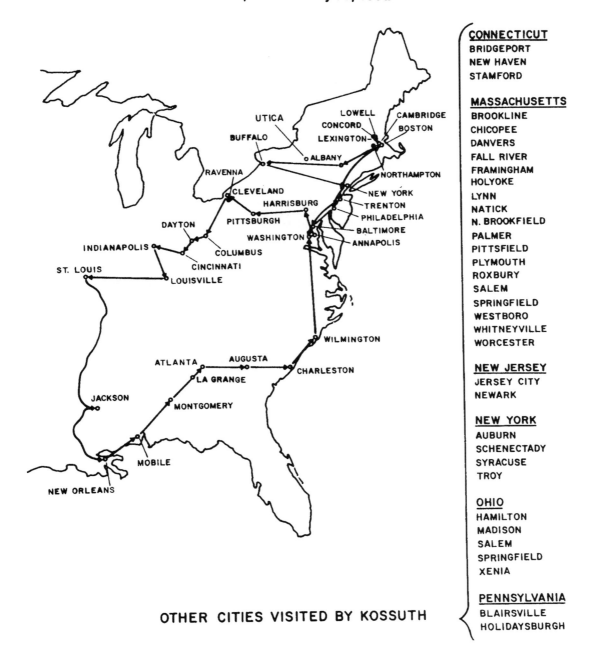

Kossuth's itinerary and map of his travel in the United States. – From the "Nation's Guest". By J. Széplaki.

LOUIS KOSSUTH'S TRIP FOLLOWED IN CHRONOLOGICAL ORDER

1851 December
- 4. Louis Kossuth arrived at Staten Island on the ship *Humboldt*.
- 6. Arrived at New York City, approx. 200,000 people greeted him.
- 11. Corporation Dinner at Irving House.
- 15. Addressed the guests of the Press Banquet.
- 16. Addressed the New York Militia.
- 17. Meeting in Tammany Hall.
- 18. Meeting in Plymouth Church, Brooklyn.
- 19. Banquet at Bar of New York.
- 21. Addressed the Ladies of New York.
- 23. Left New York for Philadelphia, where he spent the Christmas holidays.
- 25. Left Philadelphia for Baltimore.
- 30. Arrived at Washington, D. C.
- 31. Visit at the White House.

1852 January
- 3. Dinner with President Fillmore.
- 5. Reception in the Senate.
- 7. Reception in the House. Legislative Banquet.
- 12. Addressed the Legislature at Annapolis, Maryland.
- 14-17. Harrisburg, Pennsylvania, Hollidaysburg, Pennsylvania.
- 21. Blairsville, Pennsylvania.
- 22-31. Pittsburgh, Pennsylvania. Left for Cleveland, on the way stops at Salem, Ohio, and Ravenna, Ohio.

1852 February
- 4. Cleveland, Ohio.
- 6-7. Columbus, Ohio, addressed the Legislature, met with Governor Wood.
- 9. On the way to Cincinnati he stopped at Xenia, Ohio, Springfield, Ohio, Dayton, Ohio, Hamilton, Ohio.
- 9-26. Cincinnati, Ohio. Received membership from Lodge No. 133 of the Free and Accepted Masons.
- 26. Left Cincinnati for Madison, Ohio by boat.

1852 March
- 2. Indiannapolis, Indiana, addressed the Legislature.
- 3-7. Louisville, Kentucky. Left for St. Louis by boat.
- 9-16. St. Louis, Missouri. On the 16th left for New Orleans by boat.
- 21. Jackson, Mississippi, meets Governor Foote.
- 26-31. New Orleans, Louisiana.

Kossuth's itinerary of his travel in the United States (continued)

1852 April
- 3. Mobile, Alabama.
- 5. Montgomery, Alabama.
- 7-9. LaGrange, Atlanta, Augusta, Georgia and Charleston, South Carolina.
- 10. Wilmington, North Carolina.
- 13. Washington, D. C., where he visited Mt. Vernon.
- 21. Trenton, and Jersey City, New Jersey.
- 24. Newark, New Jersey. Left for New England, special train carries him to Boston. On the way he stopped at Stamford, Bridgeport, New Haven, Connecticut; Springfield, Chicopee, Holyke, Whitneyville and Northampton, Massachusetts.
- 26. Palmer, North Brookfield, Worcester, Westboro, Framingham, Natick, Brockline and Roxbury, Massachusetts.
- 27-30. Boston, Massachusetts, where he addressed the Legislature at Faneuil Hall.

1852 May
- 3. Speech at Bunker Hill.
- 4. Cambridge, Massachusetts.
- 5. Lowell, Lynn, Salem, Danvers, Massachusetts.
- 8. Boston, Massachusetts, addressed the Germans.
- 10. Roxbury, Massachusetts.
- 11. West Cambridge, Lexington, Concord, Massachusetts, where Ralph Waldo Emerson greeted him.
- 12. Plymouth, Massachusetts.
- 13. Fall River, Massachusetts.
- 14. Closing address in Boston, Massachusetts.
- 18. Pittsfield, Massachusetts, arrived at Albany, New York.
- 20. Speech at Albany, New York.
- 22. Buffalo, Niagara Falls, New York.
- 29. Auburn, New York.

1852 June
- 4. Syracuse, New York.
- 9. Utica, New York. Left for New York City, visiting en route Schenectady, and Troy, New York.
- 21. New York City, where he lectured in Broadway Tabernacle.
- 23. Addressed New York Germans.

1852 July
- 14. Sailed for England.

Kossuth's itinerary of his travel in the United States (continued)

Picture of Kossuth. The brave Hungarian tramples down Austria's eagle and Austria's crown. – From "The Nation's Guest". By J. Széplaki.

KOSSUTH, AS GOVERNOR OF HUNGARY, IN 1849.

LOUIS KOSSUTH* was born at Monok, in Zemplin, one of the northern counties of Hungary, on the 27th of April, 1806. His family was ancient, but impoverished; his father served in the Austrian army during the wars against Napoleon; his mother, who still survives to exult in the glory of her son, is represented to be a woman of extraordinary force of mind and character. Kossuth thus adds another to the long list of great men who seem to have inherited their genius from their mothers. As a boy he was remarkable for the winning gentleness of his disposition, and for an earnest enthusiasm, which gave promise of future eminence, could he but break the bonds imposed by low birth and iron fortune. A young clergyman was attracted by the character of the boy, and voluntarily took upon himself the office of his tutor, and thus first opened before his mind visions of a broader world than that of the miserable village of his residence. But these serene days of powers expanding under genial guidance soon passed away. His father died, his tutor was translated to another post, and the walls of his prison-house seemed again to close upon the boy. But by the aid of members of his family, themselves in humble circum-

---

* Pronounced as though written *Kos-shoot*, with the accent on the last syllable. The Magyar equivalent for the French LOUIS and the German LUDWIG is LAJOS. We have given the date of his birth, which seems best authenticated. The notice of the Austrian police, quoted below, makes him to have been born in 1804; still another account gives 1801 as the year of his birth. The portrait which we furnish is from a picture taken a little more than two years since in Hungary, for Messrs. GOUPIL, the well-known picture-dealers of Paris and New York, and is undoubtedly an authentic likeness of him at that time. The following is a pen-and-ink portrait of Kossuth, drawn by those capital artists, the Police authorities of Vienna:—" *Louis Kossuth*, an ex-advocate, journalist, Minister of Finance, President of the Committee of Defense, Governor of the Hungarian Republic, born in Hungary, Catholic [this is an error, Kossuth is of the Lutheran faith], married. He is of middle height, strong, thin; the face oval, complexion pale, the forehead high and open, hair chestnut, eyes blue, eyebrows dark and very thick, mouth very small and well-formed, teeth fine, chin round. He wears a mustache and imperial, and his curled hair does not entirely cover the upper part of the head. He has a white and delicate hand, the fingers long. He speaks German, Hungarian, Latin, Slovack, a little French and Italian. His bearing when calm, is solemn, full of a certain dignity; his movements elegant, his voice agreeable, softly penetrating, and very distinct, even when he speaks low. He produces, in general, the effect of an enthusiast; his looks often fixed on the heavens; and the expression of his eyes, which are fine, contributes to give him the air of a dreamer. His exterior does not announce the energy of his character." Photography could hardly produce a picture more minutely accurate

THE INTERNATIONAL MAGAZINE
Of Literature, Art, and Science.

Vol. V.   NEW-YORK, JANUARY 1, 1852.   No. I.

First page of The International Magazine of Literature, Art, and Science, Vol. 5, No.1. New York, January 1, 1852.

For the National Era.
AMERICA'S WELCOME TO KOSSUTH.
BY I. H. JULIAN.

Tune—"*Rule, Britannia.*"

Hail! Freedom's prophet, priest, and chief—
  The victim-leader of the opprest!
The land, the great birth-land of Washington,
  Exults to greet her honored guest.
      CHORUS.
God grant to thee to see — to *make* thy country free,
O, noble heart of Hungary!

The mystic splendor of thy fame—
  Thou of true heart and tireless hand—
The flowery grace, fruitful of gallant deeds,
  Hath won the admiring love of every land.
      God grant to thee, &c.

Columbia's heart-worn welcome take—
  Take, too, repentance for the past—
That when fell tyrants crushed thy father-land,
  No stern rebuke in Freedom's scale was cast.
      God grant to thee, &c.

Safely within our peace-barred gates,
  O'erwearied patriot, repose,
Till comes the hour, the long-appointed hour,
  That ends down-trodden Europe's woes.
      God grant to thee, &c.

Then go—but for attendant take
  The New World's benison of might—
Her potent word—perchance her mightier sword
  Shall aid to vindicate the Right!
      God grant to thee, &c.

But, whatsoe'er thy fate may be,
  Conqueror or captive—earth's acclaim,
Long as the human soul loves Liberty,
  Shall rend the heavens at KOSSUTH's name!
      God grant to thee, &c.

Centreville, Indiana.

America's Welcome to Kossuth. Poem, and text for a hymn. By I.H. Julian. National Era. December 11, 1851.

"Hungarian National March". Title page of the piano scores by Vincenz Czurda. – From "The Nation's Guest". By Joseph Széplaki.

The heading of The Liberator, the weekly herald of the abolitionists. Boston, April 30, 1852.

*Note the three religious and social scenes reflecting the social concerns of the period.

Statue of Lajos Kossuth in Cleveland, Ohio, restored by sculptor Csaba Kúr.

The statue of Kossuth in Cleveland, Ohio made in 1903. It was recently restored.
– From the "Dedication of Kossuth's bust". House Doc. 101–1680.

The statue of Kossuth in New York. It was erected in March 1928 by the initiation of Hungarian Americans. – From "The Nation's Guest." By Joseph Széplaki.

*It was recently restored. On its rededication in 2000, F. Mádl, the president of the Hungarian Republic was also present.

Bronze bust of Louis Kossuth presented to the Congress on March 15, 1990. – From House Doc. 101–1680.

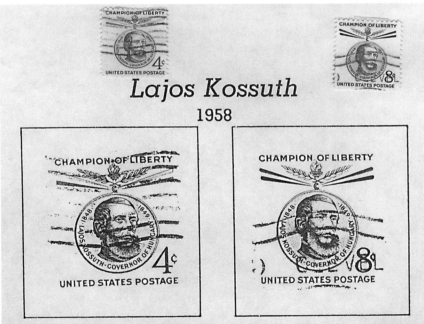

Lajos Kossuth on the "Champion of Liberty" postage stamps. 1958. – From the collection of R. Gracza.

The Liberty ship, "U.S.S. Kossuth" built during World War II. – From "The Nation's Guest". By Joseph Széplaki.

The last portrait of Louis Kossuth. Printed from the engraving of Dobi Jenő. – From the "Szabadságharcz Története" by Gracza György.